DEAD FA...

ELIZABETH I

AND HER CONQUESTS

by Margaret Simpson

Illustrated by Philip Reeve

Hippo

Scholastic Children's Books,
Euston House, 24 Eversholt Street,
London, NW1 1DB, UK

A division of Scholastic Ltd
London ~ New York ~ Toronto ~ Sydney ~ Auckland
Mexico City ~ New Delhi ~ Hong Kong

Published in the UK by Scholastic Ltd, 2001

Text copyright © Margaret Simpson, 2001
Illustrations copyright © Philip Reeve, 2001

10 digit ISBN 0 439 99823 9
13 digit ISBN 978 0439 99823 9

All rights reserved
Typeset by M Rules
Printed and bound in Denmark by Nørhaven Paperback A/S, Viborg

10

CONTENTS

INTRODUCTION

Elizabeth I is the most famous queen who has ever ruled England. Yet she almost didn't rule at all.

This argument went on for the whole of Lizzy's life. Some people got so worked up about it that they plotted to kill her. And even the people who weren't trying to get rid of her were trying to marry her off. In those days it was thought women couldn't possibly rule without a husband to tell them what to do.

Elizabeth wasn't having that.

I'M NOT DODGING ALL THOSE DEATH THREATS JUST TO HAND OVER ALL MY POWER TO SOME BLOKE.

She kept everyone guessing about her love life. Although she had loads of suitors and romantic conquests, she rejected them all in the end.

Liz didn't want the expense or violence of war, but she had one conquest in mind all through her long reign. She knew that she needed the love and respect of her people to keep her crown – and she went out of her way to conquer the hearts of her subjects.

She survived plots, smallpox, plague and war and proved to be one of the cleverest rulers this country has ever had. She was tough and sometimes unscrupulous, but above all she was strong, and by the end of her reign she was called Gloriana and England was stronger and more united than it had been for centuries.

Find out how Elizabeth kept her cool and her head through all the dangers with an exclusive look at what she might have written in her secret diary. Check out *The Tudor Tatler* for the inside scoop on all the news that was fit to print. And see what it would have been like to live in Lizzy's World.

MEET THE FAMILY

Elizabeth Tudor was born on 7 September 1533. Her dad – Henry VIII, famous for his six wives – was not pleased that she was a girl. He already had a daughter, and he wanted a son to be king after him. (Like most people of the time, Henry didn't think women were clever or strong enough to govern a country…)

Henry was fed up, but a lot of other people rubbed their hands in glee. Terrible rumours were put around Europe by people who didn't like Henry.

CHILD'S A MONSTER WITH TWO HEADS!

SERVES HIM RIGHT! WHO DOES HE THINK HE IS ANYWAY?

Why was there so much bad feeling? Let's look at Lizzy's family.

7

Dad. One of the BIGGEST and BRAINIEST kings of England. Six feet tall, red-haired, good-looking, Henry VIII was famous for his love of wine, women, song and dance. He liked his own way – and he could be very cruel about ditching people when they weren't useful to him any more.

Henry's first wife, Catherine of Aragon. A Spanish princess who had been married to Henry VIII for twenty years. Catherine had only one living daughter and Henry was getting restless. He needed a son. Even though Henry was vile to her, Catherine went on being nice to him.

Princess Mary. The only surviving child of Henry and Catherine of Aragon. Like her mother – and her father up until that time – Mary was a Roman Catholic. Roman Catholics didn't believe in divorce. Mary was a strait-laced sort of person, who got grimmer as her life went on. Then again, when you see what she had to put up with, it wasn't surprising.

Mum. Known as the 'The Midnight Crow' and 'The Witch' by her enemies, Anne Boleyn was said to be short, swarthy, with a long neck and a big mouth. She was also very pushy. She knew Henry was crazy about her, so she played hard to get. Henry wasn't used to this sort of treatment. It made her seem all the more attractive to him. He decided he would marry her – the only trouble was, he was already married, so he had to think of a way of getting rid of his Queen.

Getting rid of Catherine

So how did Henry manage to get out of his first marriage? Just a few months before Elizabeth was born, the Palace made a shocking announcement…

THE TUDOR TATLER

23 May 1533

KING'S MARRIAGE NEVER LEGAL!

After six years of begging the Pope to annul his marriage, King Henry learned today that he had never been legally married in the first place!

Newly-appointed Archbishop of Canterbury Thomas Cranmer took just four sessions to work out that Henry should never have been allowed to marry his brother's widow.

Spanish Catherine was married to Henry's big brother, Arthur, when she was fifteen years old but Arthur died five months after the wedding. Henry's dad, Henry VII, was keen on keeping the alliance with Spain, so he asked the Pope to say it was OK for the young prince to marry his brother's young widow. At that time the Pope was fine with it.

But yesterday Archbish Cranmer ruled that the Pope was wrong. Now Henry is free to marry his live-in girlfriend, Anne Boleyn. A spokesman for the Palace said that the King was delighted, but that there would be no big wedding as the King had already married Anne in a secret ceremony.

'However, Anne Boleyn will be crowned Queen of England as soon as possible,' said the spokesman. When asked whether Queen Catherine would be allowed to keep her title, he went back into the Palace for consultations. A later statement said that from now on Catherine would be called 'the Princess Dowager'.

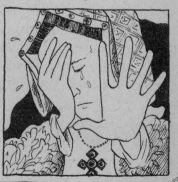

Henry didn't waste time after his divorce. He held a coronation for Anne a week later. Anne, who was very pregnant, rode in ex-Queen Catherine's barge, with her coat-of-arms nailed up where Catherine's used to be.

The people of London weren't mad about her.

In those days it was the custom for men to doff (take off) their caps in the presence of their betters. A lot of men refused to doff their hats to Anne. Some of them even booed the new queen.

. Apprentices said the whole thing was a big joke – and pointed to the initials of the King and Queen to prove it.

To marry Anne Boleyn, Henry had ditched a wife of twenty years and sacked the Pope as head of the Church in England. Lots of Englishmen and -women thought the King was way above himself. They refused to change their religion just to make Henry's new marriage legal. Others, who didn't like the Church of Rome, thought it was a good thing.

Whatever the rights and wrongs of it, the King's action set off centuries of religious conflict. Over the years, many people would be tortured and burned at the stake because they were the 'wrong' religion according to whoever was in power at the time. Henry didn't know this of course, and if he had, he wouldn't have cared. He had got what he wanted – a new young queen who could produce a lot of sons.

The baby princess

Unfortunately for Queen Anne, her first (and last) living baby was a girl. Many people said it served her right. But the baby's christening was celebrated with great splendour.

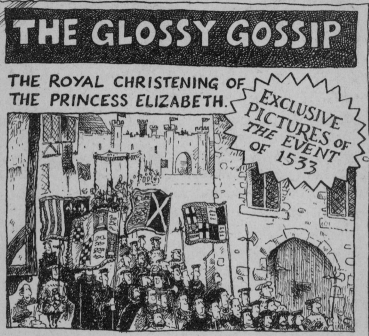

THE GLOSSY GOSSIP

THE ROYAL CHRISTENING OF THE PRINCESS ELIZABETH.

EXCLUSIVE PICTURES OF THE EVENT OF 1533

The christening procession, which snaked along for nearly a mile, as it left Greenwich Palace.

Friary Church, Greenwich, near the City of London was the scene of pageantry and rejoicing last Wednesday afternoon. A huge procession set out from Greenwich Palace to accompany the three-day-old Princess Elizabeth of England to and from her christening ceremony.

The baby princess is carried to church by her great-aunt, the dowager Duchess of Norfolk. The train of purple velvet edged with ermine was so heavy that two courtiers were needed to help lady-in-waiting the Countess of Kent.

Those lucky enough to live along the route of the procession hung tapestries from their windows and invited their friends to come and get a glimpse of the new princess.

The dowager Duchess of Norfolk, the baby's godmother, watches the Bishop of London baptize the baby princess.

Baby Bess sleeps while the adults enjoy a cup of spiced wine. 'She has her father's red hair,' said a guest.

Lizzy's christening was a big state occasion, but Dad wasn't there. Why not?

No one knows. Some people said he didn't show up because he was annoyed that his new queen had had a girl and not a boy. It's probably true. If Elizabeth had been a boy, nothing on earth would have prevented him from being there.

Someone else who wasn't at the christening was Lizzy's half-sister, Mary. She wasn't asked, but she would probably have found an excuse not to go anyway.

Poor Mary. For several years she was very unhappy. Young Queen Anne sent messages to her servants that if Mary became uppity she was to be given a good box on the ears. She wasn't allowed to see her mother, even when Catherine became ill with cancer.

Lizzy, on the other hand, had a great life. Her mum and dad came to see her often. She was a beautiful baby, with very fine clear skin and reddish hair. Queen Anne made sure she was dressed in colours that suited her – yellow and green silk and satin, made specially for her by Anne's own dressmaker.

LIZZY'S WORLD: Fit for a Princess

Who looked after Liz?
Lizzy was looked after by her Mistress of the Household, a woman called Lady Bryan, who was like a very posh nanny. She was fed by wetnurses (ladies who breast-fed the children of women posher than themselves), dry nurses (who looked after the nursery), not to mention all the men servants. She also had a governess (Kat Ashley) from an early age, as well as ladies-in-waiting. Chief lady-in-waiting was big sis Mary, who was narked because she no longer had a household of her own.

JUST YOU WAIT...

Why didn't the princesses live with their mum and dad?
That's just the way it was. Royal children had their own households in Tudor times.

Why household? What's the matter with the word house?
'Households' meant staff, from lords and ladies-in-waiting through cooks and music teachers down to

scullery maids. Houses were something else, and princes and princesses usually had more than one. Even as a child, Elizabeth had three houses: Hatfield, north of London, Eltham, south of London and Hunsdon in Hertfordshire.

Why did she need three houses?
Because the household kept moving. One reason was to give the domestic staff a rest from their normal duties ... so they had time to clean the place! Another was because a big household needed more food than one village could supply all year round. But the main reason was probably because the bogs got very smelly. There were no water closets in those days, just wooden seats over a long drop. With hundreds of people using them ... well, use your imagination!

Henry and Anne cooed over Elizabeth, but they ignored Mary – because Mary refused point-blank to say that her father was Head of the Church. This made Henry absolutely furious. Her behaviour caused the Imperial ambassador to send her a letter...

October 1535

Your Royal Highness,

I write to you as your very good friend. Word has reached me of your difficulties when the household of the Princess Elizabeth moves. I am told that you refuse to travel unless you are in your rightful place at the head of the procession.

Highness, no one believes more fervently than I that you are your father's true heir, but I beg you not to lose your dignity. It is surely better to travel behind the Princess Elizabeth with your head held high than to be dragged kicking and screaming from the house.

Pray, Highness, for your own sake, do not let such a scene occur.

I am your devoted friend and loyal servant,
Eustace Chapuys

Mary only half took the Ambassador's advice. There were no scenes where she was dragged out screaming; instead she rushed out of the house first every time so she could get right to the front of the procession.

The three most important Catholic ambassadors at court were the French ambassador; the Spanish ambassador (who represented Philip of Spain); and the Imperial ambassador (who represented his father, Charles V, and later the side of Philip's family which ruled over Austria and the Netherlands).

In 1534, Henry got parliament to pass a new Act of Succession. This said that only the children of Anne Boleyn were the legitimate heirs to the throne of England – and that he was Head of the Church, so there.

Lots of famous people refused to sign the Act of Succession. They paid with their lives.

Three Carthusian Monks were dragged through the streets of London today before being hanged, drawn and quartered.

POPE CREATES FISHER CARDINAL

The new Pope today sent word that John Fisher, Bishop of Rochester, was to be his right hand man in England. Fisher has been one of the King's most outspoken opponents in the matter of his divorce.

FISHER EXECUTED

Cardinal John Fisher, Bishop of Rochester, laid his head on the block today for his beliefs – and had it chopped off.

SIR THOMAS GETS THE CHOP

Sir Thomas More, one of the King's oldest advisers, died by the axe yesterday. He met his death calmly, pushing his long white beard and hair – he has not been able to shave in prison – out of the way of the executioner's blade.

Little Lizzy knew nothing about all this, of course. She was still in her nursery, being dressed in pretty clothes which suited her colouring, and having her big half-sister curtsey to her. But Elizabeth's life was about to change too. She wasn't going to be a royal princess for much longer.

Anne for the chop

Queen Anne was a bit of a handful – she had a terrible temper, and she liked to flirt. When she gave birth to a dead baby boy, Henry decided God was angry. He was telling him he should never have left Catherine – who by this time was dead from cancer. He decided to get rid of Anne, and start all over again.

It was a bit tricky trying to find legal grounds for this divorce. The easiest way would be to say he should never have put aside Catherine, but even Henry knew his subjects wouldn't stomach that. So he accused Anne of having other boyfriends, and said that this was treason – a crime against the state. The penalty for treason was death!

It was a stitch-up, but Anne was tried for adultery and found guilty. All the men she was accused of going off with were executed.

THE TUDOR TATLER

19 May 1536

FRENCH SWORD FOR ANNE

Anne, Queen of England, died today on the scaffold. Her execution had been delayed for two days because King Henry agreed to her request and sent for a French executioner who despatched her French-style, with a sword. It was a fitting end for a woman who was mad about all things French from fashion to food.

Anne leaves one daughter, the Princess Elizabeth. It is not yet clear where this baby will stand in the line of succession to the English throne.

Everyone apart from the lawyers forgot about poor little Lizzy. Her governess wrote to complain to Henry's advisor, Sir Thomas Cromwell...

June 1536

Dear Lord Cromwell,
Find myself a bit stuck about what to call Herself at this point. Is she still a princess? Would be good to know so I can tell the servants.

Mr Shelton (my opposite number, in charge of the men of the house) has started saying the baby should be treated no differently to anyone else, and that she should eat with everyone else. I'm not keen on this – it's not right. What if she spills her food or misbehaves? Everyone would see.

And the Princess has nothing to wear. She has outgrown all her clothes and I've no cloth nor money to buy any to make new ones.

Please help me out.
Your loyal servant,
Lady Bryan

Henry was too busy to sort out details like Lizzy's wardrobe. He was running a kingdom, not to mention wooing his next wife. He married again within a month of Anne Boleyn's death, this time a nice, shy woman called Jane Seymour who, like Anne, was a Protestant.

Jane helped Henry to make up his quarrel with his older daughter Mary. Jane was also nice to Elizabeth. And finally she even managed to give Henry what he had wanted for so long.

ELIZABETH'S SECRET ~~DAIRY~~ (Aged 4)
DIARY 16 October, 1537

I have a new baby brother. His name is Edward. He ~~was~~ was christened yesterday and I carried his christening robe.

Baby Ed's christening robe was too heavy for four-year-old Lizzy to carry on her own. She had to be carried as she held the robe by one of the gentlemen of the court.

Catholic Mary was Edward's godmother (even if he was being baptized a Protestant). And the two half-sisters walked out of the chapel hand in hand.

23

The era of Happy Families didn't last long. Little Edward had been delivered by caesarean section. In Tudor times that was not good news. Operations were brutal, with no anaesthetic. Infection set in.

ELIZABETH'S SECRET DIARY (Aged 4)

27 October 1537

Papa is very sad. Edward's Mama has died of fever, twelve days after he was born.

Henry was heartbroken. He said Jane was the only woman he had really loved. A double grave was prepared and when he died (ten years later) he was buried beside her.

LIZZY AND HER LESSONS

WHEN THAT SHE WAS AND A TINY LITTLE GIRL
WITH A HEIGH-HO, THE WIND AND THE RAIN,
STEPMOTHERS CAME AND WENT IN A WHIRL,
AND SHE HERSELF WAS ENGAGED ONCE OR TWAIN.

THERE'S NOTHING LIKE
A GOOD MINSTREL...

AND HE'S NOTHING
LIKE A GOOD
MINSTREL!

Children in Tudor times grew up quickly. Girls wore clothes just like their mums from the start; boys were dressed like their dads from the time they were six. And those children who learned to read and write – such as royal children – began very early indeed, when they were three or four years old. There were no books like *Thomas the Tank Engine* or *Harry Potter* for them, either. It was straight into the Bible and Greek philosophers. No wonder six-year-old Lizzy was described as 'grave as a woman of forty'.

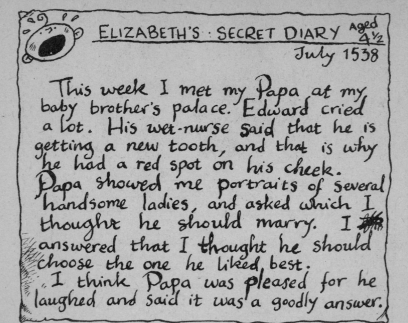

ELIZABETH'S · SECRET DIARY Aged 4½

July 1538

This week I met my Papa at my baby brother's palace. Edward cried a lot. His wet-nurse said that he is getting a new tooth, and that is why he had a red spot on his cheek. Papa showed me portraits of several handsome ladies, and asked which I thought he should marry. I answered that I thought he should choose the one he liked best. I think Papa was pleased for he laughed and said it was a goodly answer.

Yes, Henry was looking for another wife. It wasn't so much that he liked being in *lurve*, it was more that he wanted another son. People didn't expect all their children to grow up in Tudor times. For a king to have only one son was a bit of a worry. What if something happened to him?

By this time, Henry was getting on a bit and didn't want to go chasing all over Europe, so he tried choosing his next wife by mail-order.

RIFFLE FLIP

BRIDE-U-LIKE

FREE CHOPPING BLOCK WITH EVERY BRIDE!

He drew up a short-list of likely princesses and sent the court painter, Hans Holbein off to paint pictures of them.

PHEW, JUST TWO MORE TO GO...

ELIZABETH'S SECRET DIARY (Aged 6½)

April 1540

Today I met my new stepmother. Her name is Anne (like my Mama). She is a princess of Cleves. I like her very much, though she speaks very little English. I told her I was already speaking French and Italian with Mistress Kat, and she was very surprised. She does not like to sing or dance, nor play the lute or viol, which surprised me very much, for my Papa enjoys these things. But she does beautiful embroidery and she is going to teach me. She is a very quiet, serious lady and seems a little afraid of my Papa.
I have sewed a cambric shirt for little Edward.

Anne of Cleves, a German princess, was not a success with Henry VIII. He married her because he didn't want to make enemies of the German states, but he wasn't happy about it. And when Henry wasn't happy…

ELIZABETH'S SECRET DIARY (Aged nearly 7)

July 1540

My new stepmother is not to be my stepmother after all, but my aunt. Papa has said that it was all a big mistake to get married to her, and from now on she is going to be his sister. Papa said he got the shock of his life when he saw her, because she doesn't look at all like master Holbein's portrait. Actually, I think she does look quite like the portrait, but I did not dare say so to Papa, who has had his chief minister, Thomas Cromwell, put in prison for telling him Aunt Anne was very beautiful.

Aunt Anne seems quite happy to be Papa's sister. She will go on living in England. She says she likes teaching me to sew and promised that we will ride together in royal processions.

For my next wife…

Next Henry decided to go for an Anne Boleyn look-alike.

MAYBE BOLEYN WASN'T SO BAD AFTER ALL…

CHUCK

BRIDE-U-LIKE

ELIZABETH'S SECRET DIARY (Aged very nearly 7!)

August 1540

Another new stepmother! This time it is a cousin of my Mama. Her name is Katherine Howard and she was a maid-of-honour to Aunt Anne when she was queen. Mistress Kat says it bodes well for me, for Queen Katherine reminds Papa of my Mama, and he loves her as he did Mama, and that will make him more fond of me.

I wonder what happened to Mama? No one has ever really explained why they split up or why she died.

Because the new young queen, who was only nineteen, was related to Elizabeth, the little princess was given the place of honour at the royal wedding banquet.

BETTER EAT UP QUICK BEFORE HE DITCHES THIS ONE, TOO.

But once again, no sooner had she made friends with this new stepmother, than stepmum vanished off the scene. Katherine was sent to the Tower when it was discovered she'd been seeing boyfriends behind Henry's back.

ELIZABETH'S SECRET DIARY (Aged 8½)
January 1542

Queen Katherine was executed yesterday. Papa is very sad and angry about it. It seems she was flirting with all the young courtiers, and that she has made Papa look a fool in front of everyone.

But MUCH MORE IMPORTANT! I have at last discovered what happened to Mama! I overheard two of the servants talking. One said that Queen Katherine and Queen Anne were two of a kind. The other said 'Nay, but nothing was ever proved against Queen Anne'. Then she said that it was all trumped up to please the King and give him a chance to execute her!

So she was executed! I spake with Mistress Kat about what I had heard, and my good mistress looked very solemn, and said that I was full old enough now to know the truth. And she said that my father was angry with Mama for her head—

strong ways, and that he wanted a reason to put her aside and take another wife, and so charges were brought against her, none true, said Mistress Kat. My poor Mama was put to the sword. And she said that I must never ever speak of it to my Papa, for if I did he might fly into a great rage and she herself would be sent to the Tower for telling of such things.

I must never do anything which will cause problems for my good Mistress Kat, who has been like a mother to me. Yet I cannot get her tale out of my head, for I had always thought that my mother, if she was executed, must have done something very bad.

I am never going to marry.

On to the next one...

Five months later, Henry took his final wife. She was older than the others, a widow who didn't want to marry him at all.

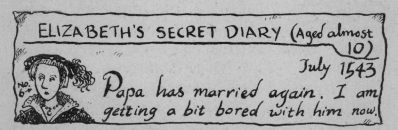

ELIZABETH'S SECRET DIARY (Aged almost 10)

July 1543

Papa has married again. I am getting a bit bored with him now.

> How many wives does he need? And how can they bear it? He is so fat and old and gross and his ulcer stinks. Poor Katherine Parr. I wonder what will happen to her?
>
> I heard the servants talking the other day, saying that she never wanted to marry him, that in her heart she is promised to Sir Thomas Seymour, but that she did not dare refuse my father, for fear she would be executed.
>
> PAPA'S STINKY ULCER →

Lizzy had what we would call a pretty disturbed childhood. She found out early on that the King could do whatever he liked, and it was dangerous to mess with him. She also learned not to tell anyone what she was really thinking.

I'M PLEASED TO SEE YOUR MAJESTY LOOKING SO HANDSOME AND HEALTHY...

HE'S THE SIZE OF A PREGNANT ELEPHANT, AND HE DOESN'T HALF PONG!

Lots of lessons

Luckily for Lizzy, there were other lessons which were more fun. She didn't go to school, but Katherine Parr, her last stepmother, organized a whole lot of tutors for young Prince Edward. Whenever Elizabeth stayed with him, she shared his lessons. Later on, Lizzy had her own tutors – Roger Ascham, who was very strict, and Thomas Gryndal, who was a lot jollier.

Monday	Tuesday	Wednesday	Thursday	Friday
Bible Study in Greek.	Bible Study in Greek.	Bible Study in Greek.	Bible Study in Greek.	Bible Study in Greek.
Classical authors: translation— Greek to English.	Classical authors: translation— Greek to English.	Classical authors: translation— Greek to English.	Classical authors: translation— Greek to English.	Classical authors: translation— Greek to English.
Classical authors: translation— English to Greek.	Classical authors: translation— English to Greek.	Classical authors: translation— English to Greek.	Classical authors: translation— English to Greek.	Classical authors: translation— English to Greek.
Lunch — Riding — Skittles				
Classical authors: translation— Latin to English.	Classical authors: translation— Latin to English.	Classical authors: translation— Latin to English.	Classical authors: translation— Latin to English.	Classical authors: translation— Latin to English.
Classical authors: translation— English to Latin.	Classical authors: translation— English to Latin.	Classical authors: translation— English to Latin.	Classical authors: translation— English to Latin.	Classical authors: translation— English to Latin.
French conversation.	Italian conversation.	Spanish conversation.	Latin conversation.	Extra Latin conversation.

Elizabeth was a real swot. Her idea for a really fun birthday present was her own personal translation of some boring religious poem. That's exactly what she sent to her stepmum – and this is the letter she sent with it. (Liz was only 11 at the time!)

> *Knowing that pusillanimity and idleness are most repugnant unto a reasonable creature, and that, as the philosopher sayeth, even as an instrument of iron or of other metal waxeth soon rusty unless it be continually occupied, even so shall the wit of a man or woman wax dull and unapt to do or understand anything perfectly unless it be always occupied upon some matter of study: which things considered, hath moved so small a portion as God has lent me, to prove what I could do.*

(Which roughly translates to: 'I'm not feeble or lazy! I know it's "use it or lose it" when it comes to intelligence. That's why I'm using what little brain I have to have a go at this translation.')

OH THANKS... YOU REALLY SHOULDN'T HAVE.

So why was Lizzy such a swot?

1 It was all the rage at the time.

Royal women throughout much of Europe were highly educated and often spoke loads of different languages. Catherine of Aragon was educated by well-known Spanish scholars and writers, and brought the custom to England. And the topics the royals studied – religion, religion, philosophy, religion, religion – were definitely the only thing anyone studied. You were dead daring – and probably Protestant – if you read a historian or a philosopher who had lived before Jesus Christ.

2 It ran in the family.

Elizabeth's great-grandmother, mother of Henry VII, translated French books into English. Lizzy's half-sister Mary was no brainbox, but even she could speak Latin, French and Spanish. Elizabeth, Edward and their cousin, Lady Jane Grey, were all brilliant at everything.

3 She was a Superbrain.

All her tutors said how brainy she was. Here's what Roger Ascham had to say:

> *Her study of true religion and learning is most eager. Her mind has no womanly weakness; her perseverance is equal to that of a man, and her memory long keeps what it quickly picks up. She talks French and Italian as well as she does English, and has often talked to me readily and well in Latin, moderately in Greek. When she writes Greek and Latin, nothing is more beautiful than her handwriting. She delights as much in music as she is skilful in it. In adornment she is elegant rather than showy.*

In other words, as well as everything else, she was a cool chick.

4 She was lonely.

Lizzy was almost always surrounded by people, but she didn't have any real friends. She was a princess, which meant everyone else was a servant. And since you couldn't safely trust anyone with what you really thought, it was much safer to read books and talk about them rather than real people.

5 She liked the attention she got for being so clever.
Poor old Lizzy had a dangerous dad. She wanted him to love her. The cover for a book that she embroidered for him one Christmas still exists. It must have taken her hours and hours.

6 There wasn't much else to do.
Well… There was no telly to veg out in front of when life got too much, so books were her only escape. But Liz would have been good at sports if she'd been at school today. She loved riding and walking and hunting, and she was also a right little raver when it came to dancing.

All change

After Henry married Katherine Parr, Lizzy's life was reasonably settled for a few years. OK, since Edward had been born, Dad had decreed that Elizabeth and Mary were both illegitimate, but he seemed to love them as much as brother Ed.

> AS IF HAVING A LITTLE BROTHER WASN'T BAD ENOUGH ALREADY.

> HA HA! I'M HEIR TO THE THRONE AND YOU'RE NOT!

LIZZY'S WORLD: The Order of Succession.

All the children of a king or queen had a place in the queue to be next ruler – 'the line of succession'. Boys always jumped to the top of the queue, even if they were babies and their sisters were grown-up.

Any royal ancestor meant that you were somewhere in the order of succession. After the children of the king came the king's brothers (in age order) and their children, then the king's sisters (in age order) and their children. Once a brother had become king then the crown passed next to his children, not his younger brother.

Because so many people had big families and married several times in Tudor England (their husbands and wives died, divorce was rare) there were usually lots of cousins and half-brothers and half-sisters kicking around with a weak claim to the throne. These folk had to ask the king or queen's permission if they wanted to get married, because by marrying another person with a weak claim, their children would have a strong one.

Children who were born to the king and his wife were higher up the queue than half-brothers and sisters whose mums weren't married to the king. So to argue about whether a king and queen were legally married meant you put a big question mark over their child's right to succeed.

This is what the royal family tree looked like:

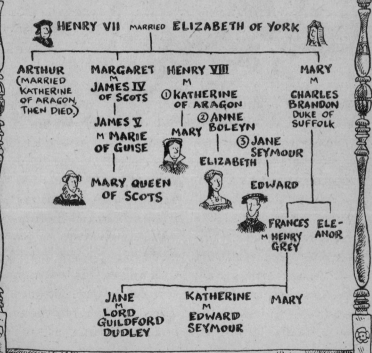

Unfortunately, Henry's health wasn't good. He had a terrible ulcer on his leg which made him cross and bad-tempered. Life was about to change for Lizzy once again.

THE TUDOR TATLER

29 January 1547

HENRY DEAD – LONG LIVE KING ED

Big bluff Henry is no more. He died after a short illness – leaving his nine-year-old son, Edward, to be King of England.

Henry collapsed a few days ago. At first courtiers hoped that he might recover, but he got worse and died in the early hours of yesterday morning.

Because Ed is so young, the country will be ruled by his uncle, Edward Seymour, Duke of Somerset (Protestant, like the young King). Somerset will head a Council of Regency until Prince Edward is old enough to rule. Somerset broke the news to the young prince and his sister, Princess Elizabeth, earlier today. Both were said to be deeply distressed at the news of their father's death.

It is understood that Henry also left a will stating that in the event of Ed dying without an heir the crown of England should pass first to his sister Mary and then to his sister Elizabeth.

Liz was staying at her house at Enfield when she was told the news of her father's death. She and Edward, who had been brought to the house to be told along with her, both burst into tears. Despite being terrified of him, they both seem to have loved their father, and they were probably scared about what would happen next. It was never an easy time when a king died leaving a child to inherit his kingdom.

AFTER HENRY

WHEN THAT SHE CAME TO HER SIXTEENTH YEAR,
WITH HEY, HO, THE WIND AND THE RAIN,
SHE LOVED AN ADMIRAL FULL OF CHEER,
BUT THE AXE IT FELL AND KILLED AGAIN.

I COULD WRITE A BETTER SONG THAN THAT, AND I'M JUST A CARTOON DOG.

One person who was secretly relieved that Henry had popped his clogs was his widow, Katherine Parr.

PHEW! I'VE SURVIVED! AND NOW I'M FREE TO MARRY THE LOVE OF MY LIFE!

The great love of Katherine's life was Thomas Seymour, brother of Edward Seymour, Lord Protector Somerset, and another uncle of the King. Unfortunately she wasn't the love of Seymour's life. He would much rather have married Elizabeth – not because he was in love with her, but because he was in love with POWER! In particular he wanted more power than his big brother.

Thom Seymour knew that his brother wouldn't allow him to marry the Lady Elizabeth. He didn't even think he'd be allowed to marry the Queen Dowager, so he did it without telling him. Then, as Thomas and Edward Seymour jostled for power, their wives argued about who should walk first in royal processions.

Katherine took Lizzy to live with her in Chelsea Palace, her house by the river Thames.

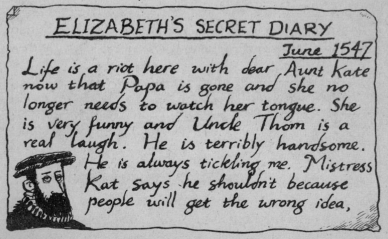

but, Uncle Thom just says, 'Don't be ridiculous woman!' It's just a bit of innocent fun!' and tickles me some more. I am always aching with laughter, screaming for him to stop, yet not wanting him to.

October 1547

Mistress Kat says that Uncle Thom behaves as he does because he is in love with me. She says that he wished to marry me, not Aunt Kate. I cannot think it is true. He is a full twenty years older than me. More, for he is eight and thirty, while I am not yet fourteen.

My cousin, Jane Grey is to come and live with us, and we shall study together.

Lord Thomas Seymour was definitely up to no good. He was flirting with Lizzy because he wanted her to be on his side against his brother – and he was using Jane too. She was a niece of Henry VIII and Lord Thomas was scheming to marry her off to King Edward. If Jane was one of 'his' people, this would give him a lot of power, he thought.

I'M JUST LORD THOMAS'S PAWN.

THINK YOURSELF LUCKY DEAR— I'M JUST HIS PRAWN.

However, things didn't go quite as Thom Seymour planned.

March 1548

To Sir Anthony and Lady Denny
Dearest friends,
I think you would enjoy a visit at Cheshunt from our dear lady, the Princess Elizabeth. This would certainly be a very good time for her to stay with you, for I find myself with child, and I think the poor girl would enjoy some livelier company.

It would be most convenient if she could leave immediately.

Your dearest friend,

K Seymour.

The real reason for Elizabeth's sudden departure was that Katherine Parr had caught the Princess Elizabeth snogging her husband. She realized things were going too far, and so she arranged for Lizzy to go and live somewhere else. Five months later Katherine died of what was known as childbed fever.

Lord Thom – free and single

♥ ELIZABETH'S SECRET DIARY ☘

October 1548

Mistress Kat keeps teasing me about Lord Thom. She says she can tell I love him for I blush when his name is mentioned, and my eyes light up when I hear men speak well of him.
She is right, though I would not

admit it for anything. Dear Aunt Kate is not long dead, and I do not wish to cause pain or scandal. But as Mistress Kat says, he is a handsome man, and will not be free long, so I should take my chance and wed him while I can.

She asked if Parry should go and speak to Lord Thom about marrying me. I did not say yes, but nor did I say no. (I hope they will take that as a yes)

I wonder what Lord Thom will say?

Thomas Parry was Liz's finance person. He did go and talk to Lord Thomas Seymour. Seymour liked the idea. Below are some thoughts he must have had around this time:

WHERE DO I WANT TO BE IN FIVE YEARS' TIME?

I WANT TO BE THE MOST POWERFUL MAN IN ENGLAND!

BUT HOW?

I COULD MARRY THE LADY ELIZABETH IF SHE WERE QUEEN I WOULD BE KING..

SHE IS SECOND IN LINE TO THE THRONE. AND EDWARD DOESN'T LOOK TOO HEALTHY TO ME...

WE WANT TO MAKE SURE MARY AND THE CATHOLICS DON'T GET INTO POWER WHEN ED POPS HIS CLOGS...

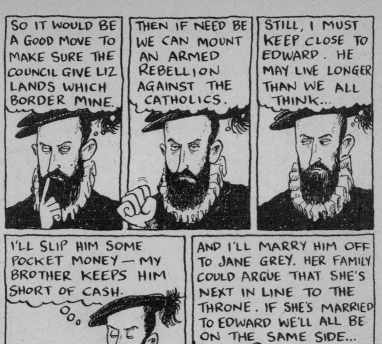

Seymour kept in with Edward by sending him pocket money. (Once he sent him £40, which was an enormous sum of money in those days.) Meanwhile he kept Jane Grey safely under his roof. Although she didn't fall for him the way Lizzy had, her family were now his allies.

He also asked different people who owned lands near his how many armed men they could muster. All in all, it looked very much as if Thomas Seymour was going to lead an armed rebellion against his brother. It wasn't long before his brother had him arrested.

The big question was, did Elizabeth know what he was up to? And was she plotting with him? If so, she was guilty of treason against the Lord Protector and her own brother, and the penalty for treason was death.

Sir Thomas Parry and Kat Ashley were taken away for questioning. Sir Robert Tyrwhitt was sent to Hatfield to interview Lizzy. He got nowhere.

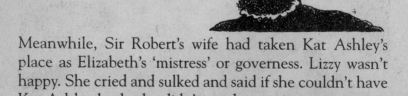

THE LADY ELIZABETH REFUSES TO ADMIT TO PLOTTING WITH MISTRESS ASHLEY AND COFFERER PARRY. SHE'S SHARP AS A NEEDLE AND I CAN'T GET A WORD OUT OF HER UNLESS I'M REALLY CRAFTY. IF YOU ASK ME THE THREE OF THEM HAVE MADE A PACT NEVER TO CONFESS.

Meanwhile, Sir Robert's wife had taken Kat Ashley's place as Elizabeth's 'mistress' or governess. Lizzy wasn't happy. She cried and sulked and said if she couldn't have Kat Ashley back, she didn't need any mistress.

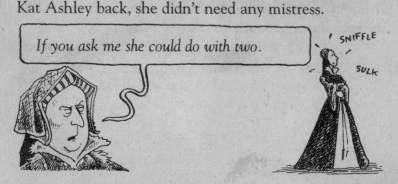

If you ask me she could do with two.

SNIFFLE

SULK

Finally, Parry gave way and admitted there had been talk of marrying Elizabeth to Thomas Seymour. But both he and Kat Ashley said Elizabeth had nothing to do with it. Lizzy herself refused to say anything to incriminate them.

Plotting to marry a princess of England without getting permission from the Lord Protector first was treason. Thomas Seymour was for the chop.

Seymour really did use dust as ink. The letters he wrote with the tip of his shoelace were smuggled out of the Tower sewn into the shoes of one of his servants.

49

He went to the scaffold, still protesting his innocence, on 20 March 1549.

When Liz heard that he had been executed, she said, 'Today there died a man of much wit and very little judgment.'

ELIZABETH'S SECRET DIARY

April 1549

I can hardly believe what has happened. Thom is dead. And I nearly followed, thanks to his boasting and foolishness. To think I actually considered marrying him! I must have been mad.

I thought he loved me. Mistress Kat said he did. He behaved as if he did. But now it seems it was all just a ruse to get power through me.

> *I must be more careful from now on. How many more men who look at me admiringly are secretly thinking how powerful it would make them to have me for a wife?*
> *I have had a lucky escape.*

For the rest of her brother's reign, Liz kept her head down and stuck to her Greek and Latin studies. Kat Ashley and Thomas Parry were released and, after a few months, allowed to return to her service. And, once the Seymour business had faded from people's memories, Lizzy was allowed to visit her brother from time to time.

There was much excitement at court today when the Princess Elizabeth arrived to visit her brother the King. With her father's golden-red hair and dressed in her customary black and white, the Princess (18) cut a striking figure among the bright silks and velvets of the court.

Liz dressed in black and white to make a point. It showed people she was a good Protestant girl. Edward's court was Protestant – he was much more extreme than his dad Henry had been – which was one reason Mary didn't like going there.

Meanwhile, Edward – who was as clever and studious as Elizabeth – was ill. He had tuberculosis, a lung disease which makes you waste away and cough up blood. As it became clear that Edward would not live long, the Protestants began to dread the day when Catholic Mary would come to the throne.

Queen Jane

Edward himself did not want Mary to succeed him – but instead of passing the crown to Elizabeth, he decided to go along with a plot by his chief minister, the Duke of Northumberland, and by-pass both his sisters. He said they were both illegitimate, and that neither of them should succeed. Instead, his cousin, Lady Jane Grey (who just happened to be married to the Duke of Northumberland's son, Guildford Dudley) should be Queen of England when he died.

ELIZABETH'S SECRET DIARY

July 1553

I don't believe it! Edward is dead and Northumberland has set aside Papa's will and proclaimed cousin Jane Queen of England instead of Mary! Now I understand why I got that message last month telling me not to come when I was riding to visit poor sick Edward.

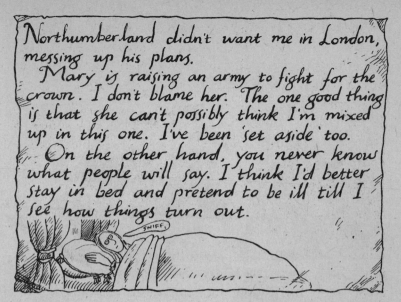

Northumberland didn't want me in London, messing up his plans.

Mary is raising an army to fight for the crown. I don't blame her. The one good thing is that she can't possibly think I'm mixed up in this one. I've been 'set aside' too.

On the other hand, you never know what people will say. I think I'd better stay in bed and pretend to be ill till I see how things turn out.

SNIFF.

It didn't take long for Mary to see off Jane Grey who had never wanted to marry Northumberland's son in the first place.

SORRY MADAM, THE CORONATION'S OFF. BUT IF YOU'D LIKE TO STEP THIS WAY, WE DO HAVE A NICE TRIAL LINED UP FOR YOU...

Elizabeth was out of bed in a flash. She rushed to London with a thousand men to swear loyalty to her sister. In fact, she got there so fast that she beat Mary to it. She was much more popular than Mary, and people flocked to see her, but Lizzy knew that if she made one false move she'd have had it.

THE TUDOR TATLER

31 July 1553

SISTERS UNITED

Today Anne Boleyn's daughter knelt before the daughter of Catherine of Aragon, and swore an oath of loyalty – to her Queen.

Queen Mary (37) arrived at the city gates accompanied by a full royal train. The Princess Elizabeth (19), who reached London two days ago, rode out to swear allegiance to her sister, accompanied by a thousand horsemen and a hundred flunkies in velvet coats.

Relations between the two daughters of Henry VIII have not always been friendly, but today it was all smiles as the new Queen raised her kneeling sister to her feet and embraced her. As the procession continued on its way towards London, Princess Elizabeth was in the place of honour immediately behind her sister.

Meanwhile, poor Jane Grey and her young husband, Guildford Dudley, and all the people accused of conspiring with them were shut up in the Tower to await trial. Among them was someone we – and Lizzy – are going to be seeing a lot more of later on – Guildford's older brother, the young and handsome Robert Dudley.

Most people were pleased that Northumberland's plot to oust Mary had failed. If anything, the plot gave her a head start, because even some Protestants thought it was safer to stick with a Catholic who was a direct descendent of Henry than start messing about with cousins just because they were Protestant. But Mary was determined to change a few things about England – and Lizzy was about to have the most difficult few years of her life.

LIZZY'S WORLD: Catholics and Protestants

Whether you were a Catholic or a Protestant Christian was incredibly important in sixteenth-century Europe – often religious differences led to war and death.

Here are some of the differences between what Catholics and Protestants believed.

Catholic beliefs	Protestant beliefs
The Pope was the direct successor of St Peter and, no matter what happened in his private life, when he spoke as Pope he was always right.	The Catholic Church and the Pope had become corrupt and did not practise what they preached. This invalidated the Pope's official pronouncements.

Ordinary people were not wise enough to decide what God wanted. They needed a priest to help them.

The Bible should be in Latin.

Priests should not marry and have children.

Bishops should wear rich robes and there should be lots of ceremony, music and incense to inspire love and awe in the congregation.

Anyone could approach God directly; there was no need for priests.

The Bible should be translated into everyday language so that ordinary people understood it.

It was fine for priests to marry and have children.

Services should be simple. There was no need for all the wealth and show of a Catholic service.

In England, the situation was even more complicated because Henry VIII was really just anti-Pope rather than properly Protestant. He just wanted his own way over divorcing Catherine of Aragon, so he made himself Head of the Church. However, when it came to church doctrine, Henry was much closer to the Catholics than he was to the Protestants. Edward, on the other hand, had been a keen Protestant, even though he was only a young boy.

Over the next hundred years the Protestants became more extreme and divided into different groups. The Puritans, for example, believed that all singing and dancing was wrong, along with church music, the theatre, nice clothes, and having a good time.

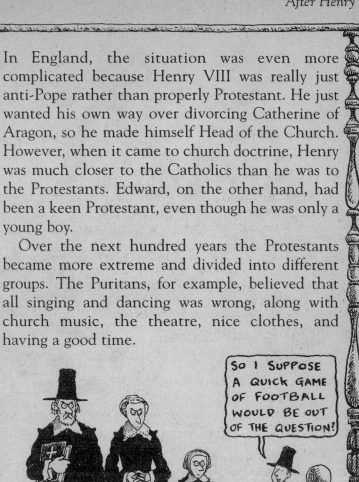

57

SISTER TROUBLE

NOW THAT HER SISTER'S QUEEN AT LAST,
TO BE R.C. IS SAFER FAR.
THE PROTS ARE OUT OF FAVOUR NOW,
AND ON THE WANE IS LIZZY'S STAR.

GERROF!

YOU'RE RUBBISH!

When Edward died and big sister Mary came to the throne, Elizabeth's troubles really began to take off.

Mary wanted to pretend that everything that had happened since her father divorced her mother hadn't really happened after all. She started by declaring Elizabeth illegitimate and saying she couldn't succeed to the throne. (Even though Henry had declared Elizabeth illegitimate too, in his will he said that Elizabeth should succeed Mary.)

Mary also wanted to say sorry to the Pope. She wanted to invite him to be head of the Christian church in England once again. And she wanted to restore the old ways of worship – Bibles only in Latin, not English. No married priests.

But in the twenty-odd years since Henry VIII had forced England to leave the Catholic church, times had changed. Lots of priests had married. People had bought church lands. They were used to reading the Bible in English. Unfortunately Mary was determined to turn the clock back. She would force everyone to be Catholic, if necessary. In fact, since she thought non-Catholics would go straight to hell when they died, Mary thought she was doing them a favour.

Mary started with the court. Everyone at court was supposed to go to Mass – including Elizabeth.

ELIZABETH'S SECRET DIARY

September 1553

Aunt Anne of Cleves and I are the only two at court who stay away from Mass. That vile Imperial Ambassador, Simon Renard, said as much to my face this morning. I know he has spoken about it with my sister, who grows ever colder towards me.

> What am I to do? If I stay away from Mass, I will be in deep trouble. Yet if I go, the Protestant lords who are now my allies may turn against me.
>
> Yet I do not need their support. In fact, better to distance myself from them, for one never knows when some hothead is going to raise a rebellion and say it is in my name.
>
> I will ask to be instructed in the Catholic faith. That will keep my sister happy.

That's what Lizzy did. She blew hot and cold, sometimes begging Mary to send her teachers who would 'put her right' on matters of religion, sometimes bunking off so that the Protestants could see that she wasn't really serious.

Mary knew that Elizabeth was just stringing her along. She didn't like Lizzy much. She knew Lizzy was more popular than she. But short of executing her – and she couldn't do that without a *very* good excuse – the only sure-fire way of scuppering Elizabeth was for Mary to have children.

The trouble was, Mary was getting on a bit. And she had never thought she was the marrying kind. But her subjects wanted her to marry and they even had an Englishman lined up for her.

Name: Edward Courtenay
Alias: Earl of Devon
Religion: Catholic
Age: 26
Height: 5'10"
Family credentials: Great-grandson of Edward IV. Father executed by Henry VIII for supporting Catholic rebellion. Mother well-known to Your Majesty, now a lady-in-waiting having been kept a prisoner in Tower of London for fifteen years.

Mary didn't want to listen to her subjects. The Holy Roman Emperor, Charles V, who was her cousin and special friend, was offering his son, Philip, who was King of Spain. Philip was young and dead dishy. Suddenly Mary discovered she *was* the marrying kind after all.

The idea of a Spanish husband did not go down well with the English people. When the Spanish envoys arrived to sign the marriage treaty nobody cheered and the London apprentice boys pelted them with snowballs.

The Wyatt plot

It was only six months into her reign, but already Mary was unpopular. Lots of people wished that Elizabeth was their queen instead of Mary. With all this bad feeling around, some of the Protestant nobles decided to make a bid for power.

December 1553

Lady Elizabeth,
I write to tell you that the news is good, with promises of arms and men from many of our supporters. We hope that you find acceptable our proposal that you marry Edward Courtenay with a view to acting as joint-sovereigns to this great realm of England.
I am, Madam, your most loyal servant,

T. Wyatt (Baronet)

Sir Thomas Wyatt, son of a famous poet of the same name, never received a reply from Liz. (Later she denied she knew anything about his plot. However, she was probably in it up to her neck. Why else did she gather a small army together?)

Unfortunately for Wyatt, Edward Courtenay – the guy Mary had turned down to marry Philip – shopped the plotters.

January 1554

Lady Elizabeth,
Betrayed by EC. Suggest you move further from London where you will be safer. Am marching on London in the morning. I might as well – I'm for the chop now unless we win. God bless you Ma'am, and may we meet in happier times.
Your most loyal servant,

T. W.

Poor old Lizzy was in deadly danger. If she ran away, she was proving she was in league with Wyatt. If she went to London to suck up to the Queen, she was abandoning an ally. Fortunately, or unfortunately, she couldn't go anywhere because she had a violent attack of kidney trouble. Maybe it was stress which brought it on. Anyway, she tossed in bed with a raging fever, her body all swollen up.

Wyatt was arrested when he reached London, but he had plenty of supporters and Mary couldn't arrest them all – especially when they were children.

THE TUDOR TATLER

5 March 1554

PHILIP 'HANGS'

It was only play, but yesterday the people of London showed what they feel about the Spanish marriage.

Three hundred schoolchildren gathered in a field and acted out a battle between the Queen and Sir Thomas Wyatt. After an hour of fierce fighting it was the Prince of Spain they hanged.

All this support for Elizabeth just proved to Mary how dangerous she was. Mary was sure she was part of Wyatt's plot. She sent her a short, sharp message.

TELL HER TO COME TO WHITEHALL AND EXPLAIN HERSELF **AT ONCE!**

RIGHTO

Lizzy was too ill to obey her sister's summons. Weak and frightened, she lay in bed and waited for news. When it came it was grim. Wyatt and other conspirators, including Edward Courtenay and Sir Nicholas Throckmorton, were under arrest and shut up in the Tower. There followed more angry messages from Mary and finally two doctors arrived to see if Liz was putting it on.

It was clear she wasn't. She was pale and weak, but – the doctors said – well enough to travel. They brought her to London in a litter. Elizabeth made them open the curtains when they reached London so that people could see her. She lay against cushions, all dressed in white, and people cheered her and wished her better.

She was brought to Whitehall Palace, and kept a long way from everyone else. The Queen refused to have anything to do with her. Simon Renard, the Imperial Ambassador, was sure that Elizabeth had been plotting against Mary and Mary listened to everything he said.

However, Liz had put nothing in writing, and so nothing could be proved. As she scratched on a window pane:

> *Much suspected of me,*
> *Nothing proved can be.*

Taken to the tower

Wyatt was condemned to death on 15th March and sent to the Tower to wait. Two days later, an armed escort arrived at Elizabeth's rooms to take her to the Tower of London. The men sent to move her had other orders too. She was not to travel through the streets, where people would see her. She was to go the Tower by river.

ELIZABETH'S SECRET DIARY

17th March 1554

When I heard what they had to say, and saw the Queen's warrant in their hands, I went cold with fear. In that moment I thought with terror of all the executions which have cut at my heart. My poor mother. Her cousin, Katherine, so young and pretty. Poor Thom who used to tickle me and make me laugh. And Jane and Guildford who were finally executed last week. And I thought: my

---

sister is too mean to build a new scaffold, she means to send me to my death on the block Jane died on.

I knew I had to delay. Anything but the Tower, for once I am there I may never come out. Either the axe will finish me or, more likely, M will have me poisoned. And so I begged pen and paper, and wrote pleading with her to believe that I had not known of Wyatt's plot. Begging her to see me. I know if I could see her, I would convince her I am a loyal sister.

When I finished the letter, I put a dozen lines diagonally across the page, so that no one should add anything and pretend it was from me.

By then it was late and, as I knew it would, the tide had turned, so it was no longer safe to sail beneath London Bridge. So, I have delayed my fate until at least tomorrow. By which time Mary will have my letter — pray God she will believe me. Pray God she will be merciful. Else I think my end is near.

67

When Mary heard that Elizabeth had managed to miss the tide, she was furious with the escort for allowing her to write the letter. She sent a message telling them to get on with what they had been sent to do.

THE TUDOR TATLER

18 March 1554

PRINCESS TAKEN TO TOWER!

All-English Princess Elizabeth was rowed to the Tower today in a covered barge – on the orders of her sister Queen Mary.

Despite her protests, Elizabeth was forced to disembark from the barge at the Tower. She pushed aside the offer of a cloak to shield her from the driving rain, and sat down on the wet steps, refusing to go in.

One of her servants, scared she was going to her execution,

burst into tears. Elizabeth was angry, and told him he should be comforting her, not the other way round.

Finally a soaked princess could take no more. She gave in and entered the Tower.

When asked how long the Princess would be staying, the Constable of the Tower of London refused to comment.

Famous prisoners currently in the tower include Sir Thomas Wyatt (under sentence of death) and Sir Robert Dudley. The Queen's cousin, Lady Jane Grey and her husband, Guildford Dudley, vacated their rooms last month when they went to the scaffold.

Elizabeth's door was not locked, but she was not allowed to communicate with anyone – none of the other prisoners, and no one outside. When she asked for pen and paper she was refused them. Mary had made it very clear that...

Lizzy lived in terror that Mary would have her killed. She knew that Wyatt was still alive and still being questioned, along with all the other conspirators. Who knew what someone might say under torture?

Finally, on 11 April, Wyatt was executed.

The news of Wyatt's gallows speech spread round London like wildfire.

THE TUDOR TATLER

13 April 1554

PILLORIED!

Londoners were angry yesterday when two men were put in the pillory for spreading rumours.

Jack Turner (43) and Giles Butcher (27) were found guilty of saying that Sir William Wyatt, executed two days ago for treason, had said the Lady Elizabeth had nothing to do with his uprising and should not be imprisoned in the Tower.

Sentenced to stand in the pillory for a day, they had many supporters who stood by to make sure that no rotten veg or stones were flung at them.

'They are being pilloried for speaking the truth,' said an elderly man who refused to be named. 'The fact is they're right. Lady Elizabeth should not be in the Tower. The Queen should let her go and beg her mercy.'

WYATT'S HEAD TWICE-LOST

The severed head of Will Wyatt disappeared from its spike on the scaffold yesterday. All guards are being questioned about the theft, which is thought to be by one of his many supporters.

SIR NICK - NOT GUILTY!

Londoners were jubilant yesterday when a jury acquitted Sir Nicholas Throckmorton of being involved in the Wyatt conspiracy. It took the jury of twelve good men and true just three hours to decide that there was not sufficient evidence to convict the knight, who was released from the Tower.

Mary knew that if the jury had acquitted Throckmorton, there was no chance of convicting Elizabeth, whatever the Spanish ambassador told her. But she still kept Lizzy in the Tower, while she decided what to do next.

As the weeks went by, Lizzy found it really hard, being shut in without her books or pen and paper. She asked to be allowed somewhere to exercise and was allowed to walk up and down a gallery, but with the shutters closed so that no one could see her. In the end, she complained so much that she was allowed to go into a small, enclosed garden. There a small boy used to visit her and bring her flowers – until Sir John Gage found out. He thought someone might try to smuggle a message to her via the small boy, and so the child's visits to the garden were stopped.

ELIZABETH'S SECRET DIARY

May 1554

So good to be able to write again. Only a week ago I was in absolute terror. I heard the sound of marching feet and looked out to see a squadron of soldiers. Began to shake, so frightened was I that they had come for my execution. I had heard no hammering of scaffolds, so I asked if Jane's scaffold still stood and was told no, it had been taken down. Then what are the soldiers come for, I asked. It was the new governor's escort, my guard told me. Who is that? I asked, and was told Sir Henry Bedingfield.

I did not know the name. I asked if he were a man of principle, for I thought perhaps he had been appointed expressly to murder me quietly, so I need never come to trial. I was told he was a good man, one who goes by the rules.

Bedingfield was an honest man, but very strict with Liz. He wouldn't allow her to do anything until he had permission in writing from the Queen or her ministers. And he had with him John, Lord Williams of Thame, who liked Elizabeth and would become a good friend to her. Mary had relented a little. Bedingfield and Williams were going to take Liz to Woodstock – and stay at Williams's house on the way.

18th May 1554

Dearest wife,

I write to you from Windsor, where I spend the night with Bedingfield and the Lady Elizabeth. Tomorrow, or the day after at latest, we will be with you. I beg you prepare a fine welcome for her. She is a clever young lady, but quite terrified. Not surprising, since no one tells her what is going on. I think she lives in constant fear that someone will do away with her. Bedingfield had told her nothing of her departure. The first she knew of it was when I arrived with a litter for her and a hundred men. She looked at me with such scared eyes as she climbed into the litter. 'This night I think to die,' she said. I longed to put an arm around her and tell her she was bound for Woodstock, but Bedingfield was standing by, and so I said simply that nothing dreadful was going to happen to her: she was safe with me.

The Lord alone knows how but by the time we reached Windsor it seemed the whole world knew we had the princess with us. People lined the lanes, and passed food into the litter, and threw posies, and shouted 'Long live Your Royal Highness!'

'Would they do this if I were going to die?' she asked me, as we disembarked her at Windsor.

I seized my moment and told her she was not going to die, or not by the axe or poison. 'You are bound for Woodstock,' I told her. 'And tomorrow you will sleep in my own house, and eat at my table.'

So make ready dear wife. I send this to you post-haste.

Your loving husband,

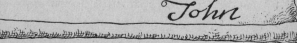

John

After staying at Williams's house at Thame, the party moved on to a dilapidated royal palace at Woodstock. Elizabeth was still under house arrest, and not allowed to write to the Queen, but she was alive and out of the dreaded Tower. There wasn't enough room for her servants in the house so they stayed at the Bull Inn. Sir Henry Bedingfield was all hot and bothered by the amount of coming and going. He was scared there was another plot being hatched right under his nose.

Philip of Spain – Elizabeth's new ally

Two months later, Mary met her fiancé Philip and fell madly in love. The feeling wasn't mutual. Philip did his duty and married Mary, but he didn't fancy her.

Philip wanted to meet Elizabeth, whom everyone said was much more fun. Mary said no, but Philip kept insisting. It wasn't just curiosity. Mary was an old woman by Tudor standards. If she did manage to get pregnant, she might well die in childbirth. Then Elizabeth would be queen, and Philip's father the Emperor Charles V was very anxious that she remain Spain's ally.

Finally Mary agreed, and Lizzy was brought to Hampton Court.

ELIZABETH'S SECRET DIARY

15 April 1555

Amazing news! After days of seeing no
one, a lady-in-waiting appeared this
evening with a beautiful gown which
she bade me put on. She said my
brother-in-law was coming to see me.
At first I could not think who she
meant, it is so hard to imagine Mary
married.

I dressed, and she did my hair, and
then I waited for some half hour until
Philip arrived. He is rather good-looking,
blond and bearded. I curtsied deeply to
him and he gave me his hand to kiss
and raised me to my feet. We spoke
for some time; I begging him to assure
my sister that I had no part in the
Wyatt rebellion, he telling me
that she expects a child in the
early summer next year. I
think he must have seen the
surprise in my face, and I
swear he raised an eyebrow
as if to say that he too found
the news unlikely. But
nothing was said, and we spoke of other
matters, of how he liked his wife's country
(well) and when he must leave to see his
other realms.

I think he was quite taken with me. He said
that he will try to press my case with my sister.

It wasn't too long after this that Lizzy had to put on her posh frock again. She was led across the garden when it was dark and no one would see, and shown into the Queen's apartments. There she fell on her knees before Mary. Philip was listening behind a screen, just to make sure that Mary really did make peace with Liz.

The interview was over. Elizabeth was no longer under house arrest – but Mary still did not trust her.

Mary's baby was due in June. By August, when she still hadn't delivered, people were laughing at her behind her back. Now it seems likely that she was never pregnant in the first place. Historians think she had a cyst or cancer which stopped her periods and made her swell up.

Lizzy was probably relieved. No baby meant she was still next in line to the throne.

Philip was desperate to get abroad. By this time he couldn't stand his wife who was still madly in love with him. He left for the continent in August and was gone for months – but he still continued to help Lizzy and protect her from his sister's anger.

Philip's main concern was to stop England ganging up with France against Spain. France and Spain were sworn enemies. At that time, the heir to the French throne was married to Mary Queen of Scots, a cousin of Elizabeth and Mary. If anything happened to Liz then Mary Queen of Scots would be next in line to the throne of England.

OOOH, I DON'T FANCY THAT...

So, if Philip wanted to be sure England kept out of French hands, he had to help keep Liz alive *and* cultivate her friendship with Spain for when she became queen.

Elizabeth was allowed to go home to Hatfield in August. She was a free woman, but she still lived under a shadow. Would one of her supporters get her into trouble? People were getting more and more restless under Mary. She had now started trying people who were not Catholics for heresy, and having them burned alive at the stake. Things got so bad that Mary was nicknamed 'Bloody Mary'.

Liz guessed that Part II of Philip's plan was to marry her off to an ally of Spain. In 1556 she was summoned to court and ordered to marry the Duke of Savoy. When she said no, Mary said she would lock her up in the Tower again.

It turned out to be only a threat, but Liz took it seriously. She was so scared that she wrote to the French ambassador, asking if she could come and live in France. He told her to sit tight: that if she wanted to inherit the English throne she should stay exactly where she was.

THAT'S IF I CAN MANAGE TO OUTLIVE MARY...

Time was on Lizzy's side. Mary was increasingly ill, and soon would be dying. She hated her half-sister more than ever by this time, and went round saying that Henry VIII wasn't Elizabeth's dad and that Elizabeth was the child of one of Anne's other boyfriends. It looked as if Mary was going to override her father's will and name someone else as her successor. The main candidates were Mary Queen of Scots and Lady Katherine Grey (Jane Grey's sister), who were both nieces of Henry VIII. From Mary Tudor's point of view, Mary Queen of Scots was the best bet because she was Catholic but Philip still wanted to avoid the Queen of Scots with her French king husband.

Philip was away as much as possible. Mary felt everything would be all right if only he would stay at home. But he didn't love Mary and only came back when he wanted England to join in his war against France. Mary was so nuts about Philip that she agreed. This cost the government a fortune, a lot of men were killed, and England's last base in France, the town of Calais, fell to the French. Mary was hated more than ever.

By this time she did not have long to live, but she still hoped she was pregnant so that she could stop Elizabeth succeeding her. Nobody else thought it was likely to happen.

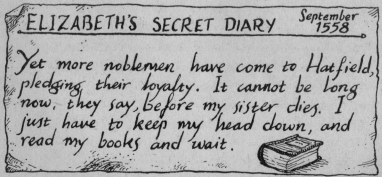

ELIZABETH'S SECRET DIARY   September 1558

Yet more noblemen have come to Hatfield, pledging their loyalty. It cannot be long now, they say, before my sister dies. I just have to keep my head down, and read my books and wait.

Yet I long for it to be over. To be queen. Can she stop me now? I have so much to thank Philip for. If he were not her husband – if she did not love him so much – I swear she would rather see the Queen of Scots on the English throne.

Have the crown of England.

Och ta very much!

I have Philip on my side. And my father's will. And the fact that the English people say that I am all English-woman, which is true. But I won't believe I'm Queen of England till it really happens.

Elizabeth wasn't just keeping her head down. She was making detailed plans for how she would govern England. And in November 1558, sure enough, she got a letter from Mary...

November 1558

Dear Elizabeth,
I fear that I do not have long to live. Despite your irregular birth I am prepared to allow you to succeed to the throne of England on the following conditions:
1) that you retain the Roman Catholic faith in England and do not revert to Protestantism.
2) that you take over all my debts.
Please let me know if you agree to these conditions.

Mary Regina

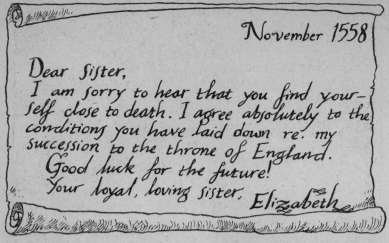

November 1558

Dear Sister,
I am sorry to hear that you find yourself close to death. I agree absolutely to the conditions you have laid down re: my succession to the throne of England.
Good luck for the future!
Your loyal, loving sister, Elizabeth

ELIZABETH'S SECRET DIARY
November 1558

Who does she think she is? She can't do anything about what I do after she's gone.
But it looks as if the crown's in the bag!

URK

Two days later, Mary fell into a coma. Ten days later she was dead. The Privy Councillors, who for centuries had been the people who ruled the country when there was a crisis, rode for Hatfield House. Elizabeth – who had probably heard the news already – was seated under an oak tree in the grounds with her nose in a book.

She was 25 and Queen of England – but it had been a close-run thing.

LIZZY'S WORLD: Little England.

When Liz came to the throne England was just a little tiddler of a country, surrounded by some much more powerful neighbours.

Until recently, Europe had been dominated by the Holy Roman Empire which took in all the Catholic countries stretching from Naples, Sicily and Spain in the south through Austria to Germany and the Netherlands in the north. Now Philip's dad, Charles V, decided it was all too much and divided it up between his sons. He gave Spain to Philip to rule, Ferdinand became Holy Roman Emperor after his dad retired to a monastery, and Charles became Archduke of Austria. Between them, the three brothers had Europe pretty well sewn up.

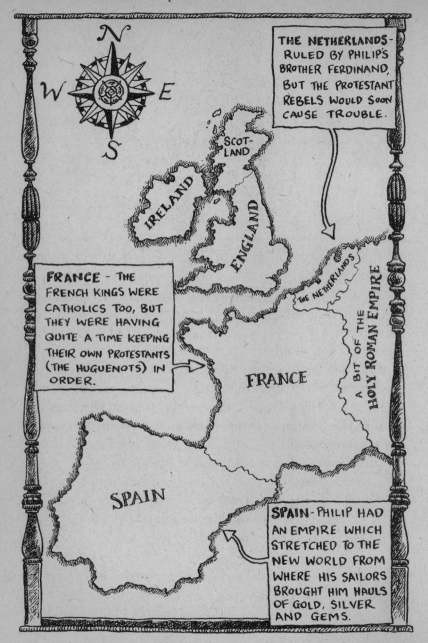

N
W E
S

THE NETHERLANDS-
RULED BY PHILIP'S
BROTHER FERDINAND,
BUT THE PROTESTANT
REBELS WOULD SOON
CAUSE TROUBLE.

SCOT-
LAND

IRELAND

ENGLAND

THE NETHERLANDS

A BIT OF THE
HOLY ROMAN EMPIRE

FRANCE - THE
FRENCH KINGS WERE
CATHOLICS TOO, BUT
THEY WERE HAVING
QUITE A TIME KEEPING
THEIR OWN PROTESTANTS
(THE HUGUENOTS) IN
ORDER.

FRANCE

SPAIN

SPAIN - PHILIP HAD
AN EMPIRE WHICH
STRETCHED TO THE
NEW WORLD FROM
WHERE HIS SAILORS
BROUGHT HIM HAULS
OF GOLD, SILVER
AND GEMS.

QUEEN AT LAST!

Elizabeth knew she was in for a rough ride when she became queen. There were many people in and out of her kingdom who thought she had no right to the throne. And most of the people who supported her thought she was only a silly young woman, and would be easily pushed around.

Liz knew she could prove them wrong, but she also knew she needed the love of the ordinary people. That meant none of the horrible cruelty that had gone on in her father's reign and in Mary's. She made her own secret resolutions...

I. I will rule over the realm of England, which Almighty God has appointed me to rule and no other country. I do not wish to conquer any other country.

II. I will not support any rebel against the rightful king of another country.

III. I, not the Pope, will be head of the Church in England. However, I am not going to be bossed around by Protestant extremists either.

IV. I will not make windows in men's souls. Loyalty to the crown matters more than what a man believes in his heart.

V. I will avoid war, which is costly of men and money, and which my country cannot afford.

VI. I will avoid executions.

VII. I will make my councillors obey me.

VIII. I will never fall in love or marry.

IX. I will keep these resolutions secret in my heart and never let anyone know what I am really up to.

The last resolution was the only one that Elizabeth was able to stick to absolutely and completely. All her life she kept her councillors, and everyone else, guessing about what she really thought. Her motto was: *Video et taceo* – I see and keep silent.

A new queen at court

Elizabeth was a shrewd judge of character. She had seen both her brother and sister make mistakes, and she had had a long time to plan what she would do differently. By the time the Privy Councillors arrived and found her under the famous oak tree, the man she had made her Secretary of State was already at Hatfield and busy at his desk. He was Sir William Cecil, a Protestant who had kept his head down under Mary. He didn't come from one of the powerful – and dangerous – noble families with a claim to the throne, but he was hardworking, careful and loyal and Liz trusted him. Although they would often quarrel, he never let her down.

Now there was a Protestant queen, it was all change again at court.

IN...

THOMAS PARRY-TREASURER TO THE HOUSEHOLD.

KAT ASHLEY-MISTRESS OF THE MAIDS OF HONOUR.

ROBERT DUDLEY-MASTER OF THE HORSE.

LORD WILLIAMS OF THAME-PRESIDENT OF THE WELSH MARCHES. (HER DELIVERER FROM THE TOWER.)

ROGER ASCHAM-LATIN SECRETARY TO THE QUEEN. (HER CHILDHOOD TUTOR & CLEVER INTELLECTUAL.)

OUT...

SIR HENRY BEDINGFIELD-FORMERLY KEEPER OF THE TOWER OF LONDON.

BISHOP BONNER-PERSECUTOR OF PROTESTANTS.

ALL QUEEN MARY'S LADIES-IN-WAITING.

BOO HOO!

WAS IT SOMETHING WE SAID?

After she had made these, and other, appointments, Liz moved to London. Stopping everywhere, she went to talk to rich and poor, old people and children. She made conquests everywhere she went. She was always doing things that her stuffier councillors thought she shouldn't. Here's what one eyewitness wrote about her.

> *If ever any person had either the gift or the style to win the hearts of people, it was this queen... All her faculties were in motion ... her eye was set upon one, her ear listened to another, her judgement ran upon a third, to a fourth she addressed her speech; her spirit seemed to be everywhere, and yet so entire in herself as it seemed to be nowhere else. Some she pitied, some she commended, some she thanked, as others she pleasantly and wittily jested, condemning no person, neglecting no office...*

She went back to visit the Tower of London. This time she rode up to the main entrance with trumpets sounding and everyone cheering.

Some have fallen from being princes of this land to be prisoners in this place. I am raised from being a prisoner in this place to be a prince of this land.

TO DO LIST.
- Bury Mary.
- Work out how to pay her debts.
- Get up to speed with Privy Council business.
- Arrange coronation: Get coronation robes altered to fit. Choose Archbishop. Send out invites. Work out route etc.
- Keep fit.

All her life, Elizabeth had a strong respect for the rights of kings and queens, even when they were personal enemies. It was as if she knew that one day she herself would need loyal subjects. So even though she had not got on with Mary, and didn't go to the funeral herself, she made sure she had a regal, Catholic send-off. She didn't want to encourage disrespect for royalty.

WOULDN'T IT BE MORE RESPECTFUL IF SHE WAS INSIDE THE COFFIN?

THAT'S JUST AN EFFIGY, YOU TWIT...

Next she had to tame the Privy Council. They were all men, and to a man they assumed that she would be useless at government. Liz decided to show them different. She went to their meetings every day, and when they had all given their opinions, she would give hers. She was proud and bossy and no one ever knew what she would do or say next.

ELIZABETH'S DAILY SCHEDULE

7 A.M. SMART WALK IN THE PALACE GROUNDS.

8 A.M. BREAKFAST.

9 A.M. AUDIENCE WITH SECRETARIES – SIGN LETTERS.

10 A.M. WORK ON STATE PAPERS, THEN MEET WITH PRIVY COUNCIL.

BLAH BLAH BLAH

11.30 A.M. DANCING!

12 NOON. DINNER.

2 P.M. MEET FOREIGN AMBASSADORS.

5 P.M. STATE BANQUET/ PRIVATE SUPPER WITH MUSIC AFTERWARDS.

8 P.M. STATE PAPERS.

12 MIDNIGHT. BED.

ZZZZZZ

LIZZY'S WORLD: A Palace Tour.

The monarch in Tudor England had three sorts of room, or chamber.

- The Presence Chamber was where the monarch made his or her public appearance in front of the whole court.
- The Privy Chamber was only open to ambassadors and people who needed a semi-private place in which to talk to the monarch.
- The Withdrawing Chambers were where the monarch lived out the private aspects of his or her life. These included the bedroom, bathroom (when there was one) and private sitting rooms.

Coronation triumph

Elizabeth had a row with a bishop on the first Christmas morning of her reign. In the royal chapel, the Bishop of Carlisle raised the Host or communion bread high up for everyone to worship it. This was the Catholic way of doing things. Liz shouted out, 'Lower that vessel at once!' The Bishop just held it higher, so the Queen stormed out.

YOU CAN PUT IT DOWN NOW, SHE'S GONE.

Because of this row, Liz had a problem finding a bishop to crown her at her coronation. In the end the Bishop of Carlisle, the one who had been shouted at, agreed.

Elizabeth had asked her favourite astrologer, Dr John Dee, to tell her the most favourable date for her coronation. He told her it was 15th January 1559.

THE GLOSSY GOSSIP

CORONATION!

SOUVENIR EDITION 17 January 1559

Two days of celebration came to a glorious climax on Saturday with the crowning of the beautiful redheaded Queen Elizabeth I in Westminster Abbey.

On Thursday, the young Queen went by water to the Tower, where traditionally the monarch spends the nights before his or her coronation. Throughout Thursday the city was made ready. Wooden rails were set up along the streets, and hung with brightly coloured cloths.

Friday morning dawned cold and bright. There was a thin sprinkling of snow on the ground. The streets were packed with well-wishers from early morning. Some of them had slept in the street in order to secure a good vantage point from which to see the coronation procession.

The Queen travels to her coronation in an open litter. Behind her rides her Master of Horse, Sir Robert Dudley.

The Queen is accompanied by her bodyguard, with the letters ER blazoned on their crimson coats.

City merchants line the streets to greet their new Queen as the City Recorder offers a crimson satin purse to the Queen containing a thousand gold coins.

The Queen stops at Fleet Bridge to receive a bunch of rosemary from a poor old woman. The herb was still in the litter when it arrived at Westminster.

The coronation procession pauses to watch one of the many pageants put on by the citizens of London.

People crowd in on the Queen as she steps from her litter at Westminster Abbey. The Countess of Lennox (back left) was nearly knocked over in the crush as she carried the Queen's train.

The Archbishop holds the crown high over Elizabeth's head and pronounces her Queen of England. For the first time ever, the coronation oath is read from an English Bible.

A cheerful Queen, in full regalia, carrying the sceptre and orb, chats to members of the congregation outside the Abbey.

The streets are swept clean after the royal procession has disappeared into Westminster Hall for a state banquet lasting many hours.

Elizabeth's coronation was a huge success. She enjoyed being out and about among the people, and they adored her. The only trouble was she caught a bad cold and had to stay in bed for a few days afterwards.

Her next Big Date was the opening of Parliament. Parliament had been going for three hundred years when Elizabeth came to the throne. Its original job had been to bring suggestions, or bills, to the King. If the King agreed to them they became Acts of Parliament.

Their big hold over the sovereign was cash. He – or in this case, she – could not raise taxes without their agreement. And if MPs didn't like what he or she was doing, they wouldn't vote for the tax, and the King or Queen would be left without funds.

As well as this, MPs had become quite keen to have a proper say in ruling the country. And Liz's first Parliament had some very definite ideas about a very important subject.

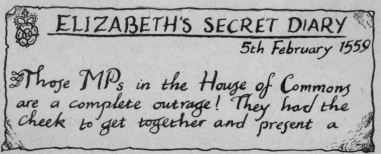

ELIZABETH'S SECRET DIARY
5th February 1559

Those MPs in the House of Commons are a complete outrage! They had the cheek to get together and present a

> speech telling me I ought to marry and breed! The nerve! What makes them think they have the right? If God had meant them to rule the country, he would have made them King. But He didn't. He made me Queen, ergo, He thinks I know best. Which I do. I am going to rule and their job is to give me the money I need to do it.
>
> I told them where to get off. Said that I had turned down marriage even when Mary was threatening to top me and that if I'd thought they were trying to give me orders, I'd be mightily offended. That so far as I could see the single state was best for me and England and that I meant to live and rule and die a virgin.
>
> So they can like it or lump it.

The men in the House of Commons (there were no women MPs at that time) were not too pleased, but they assumed that sooner or later the Queen would change her mind. They weren't the only ones who thought Elizabeth should marry. In those days, no one thought a woman could rule on her own, not even Lizzy's top adviser, William Cecil.

Did she mean it?

Elizabeth kept on saying that she would never marry. Well, did she mean it? And if so, why?

Reasons for Marriage

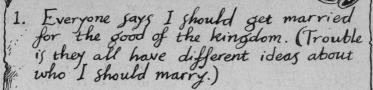

1. Everyone says I should get married for the good of the kingdom. (Trouble is they all have different ideas about who I should marry.)

2. I need an heir. (But I might die in childbirth like poor Jane Seymour or dear Aunt Katherine. Then there would be a Regency or, worse, pesky cousin Mary would succeed me.)

Hooray!

Reasons against Marriage

1. I might make a mistake. After all, Dad made quite a few.

2. Men are only after one thing. (My crown.) Even darling Thom Seymour was interested in power, not me.

3. My subjects may want me to marry, but they won't like it if I marry a foreign king or prince. Look what happened to Mary. All those foreigners roaming the streets and then we get involved in Spain's wars.

4. If I marry one of my own subjects the others will be jealous and gang up on him.

5. Anyway, I haven't seen half of these guys, and I'm definitely not choosing a husband from his portrait. I might end up with someone really hideous. Look at Dad when he saw poor Aunt Anne. Or Philip when he saw sister Mary, come to that.

6. By staying single, I can keep everyone guessing. So long as I never make up my mind, they'll all think they're in with a chance. That way their governments will be nice to England.

CONCLUSION

No way will I get married.

Whatever she said, the young Queen of England was thought to be the best marriage prize in all Europe. At one stage in 1559 there were *ten* ambassadors all hoping to woo her for their master! Here's what happened to a few of her most important suitors.

1 King Philip of Spain

Yes, this was the same Philip who had been married to her sister, but so what? He needed a wife, and he needed an alliance with England, so Elizabeth – who was younger and prettier than Mary – fitted the bill nicely. He offered to marry her provided she became a Catholic.

Liz told the Spanish ambassador she would have to get permission from Parliament. (She never asked them.)

Then she started quoting all Philip's own doubts back to the ambassador. (Her spies had read Philip's letters to the ambassador.) She said…

I'D LOVE TO MARRY YOUR MASTER, BUT IT WOULDN'T BE RIGHT. AFTER ALL, I'M A HERETIC.

IS SHE TAKING THE MICK?

But the next time the ambassador came, he told Liz that Philip had married a *different* Lizzy – Princess Elisabeth of France, who was only fourteen. (He had decided to get France on his side.)

I'M AFRAID YOUR GRACE HAS ONLY YOURSELF TO BLAME FOR KEEPING MY MASTER WAITING.

YOUR MASTER CAN'T HAVE BEEN VERY MUCH IN LOVE IF HE GAVE UP AFTER ONLY FOUR MONTHS.

SHE CAN'T BE… SHE *IS*! SHE'S LAUGHING AT ME!

TEE HEE HEE!

HA HA!

SNORT.

TITTER!

GIGGLE!

> *What can be said here to Your Majesty is only that this country ... has fallen into the hands of a woman who is a daughter of the Devil, and is one of the greatest scoundrels and heretics in the land.*

SCRITCHETY SCRITCH SCRATCH SCRITCH

2 Prince Eric of Sweden

Eldest son of the King of Sweden, Eric was crazy about Elizabeth and he had the advantage of being a Protestant. He sent his handsome brother, Duke John of Finland, to woo her. Liz got on so well with him that people thought she might marry him instead of Eric. Don John liked England and gave big presents to various courtiers, hoping to impress them. (A lot of the money he gave turned out to be forged!) Elizabeth turned down Eric in May 1559, but two months later he was writing to her that he would go through wind and storm to be with her. A year later he did – and his fleet was blown apart. He had to turn back. Still he wouldn't give up. In the end Lizzy said 'No' four times.

3 The King of Denmark

The Danish king's envoy had a great idea. He pranced around the court wearing a velvet doublet with a pierced heart on it. It didn't do him or his master any good with Liz.

4 Archduke Charles of Austria

Charles was the main contender, even if there is a bit of confusion here. Philip II of Spain had two brothers, Ferdinand and Charles. In the end, the Imperial ambassador pushed forward Charles who was less religious than his brother, and so less bothered about the fact Elizabeth was a Protestant.

His father, the retired Charles V, thought…

I WOULDN'T LET HIM PUT HIS SOUL IN DANGER IF SHE WASN'T SUCH A GOOD CATCH.

Liz kept the Archduke Charles on a string for ages. One night when the Imperial ambassador was about to give up hope, he met the Queen in her barge on the river. The two barges drew alongside, Lizzy invited him aboard, played the lute to him and let him think that Charlie was in with a chance. He wasn't really...

LIZZY IN LOVE

THE TUDOR TATLER

April 1559

THE KISS!

The picture the world's been waiting for – the Queen of England embraces her Master of Horse.

While ten ambassadors attend court, competing for the Queen's hand in marriage, Elizabeth has decided to take time out from governing the country and have herself a good time. Rumours have been flying for weeks now linking flighty Elizabeth with hunky married man, Rob Dudley, 29.

Rob is exactly the sort of sporty type Elizabeth likes – tall, handsome, witty, an expert horseman and a keen jouster and dancer – a bit like her old man, Henry VIII, in fact. And the couple have known each other since they were children. They were even imprisoned in the Tower at the same time, though friends say they never met there.

As the Queen's Master of Horse, Rob gets to go riding or hunting with Elizabeth every day, and recently, say friends, their friendship has blossomed into love.

Not everyone thinks she's made a wise choice. Rob's dad and his grandad were both executed for treason, and he's a married man.

But she may not have to wait long – Amy Dudley, who lives apart from her husband – is said to be dying of breast disease.

Judging by the picture, taken last night at a court ball, Amy's the last thing on the Queen's mind.

Yes, the Virgin Queen had got caught out by her hormones. She was in love. As Liz and Rob became closer and closer, tongues began to wag – not just in London but all over Europe.

Lord Robert has come so much into favour that he does whatever he likes with affairs and it is even said that Her Majesty visits him in his chamber day and night...

AND WAIT TILL SHE HAS THE BABY!

BABY? THERE'S NO BABY!

NOT YET. BUT THEY'VE PUT ONE IN THE MAKING.

Mother Annie Dowe, of Brentwood in Essex, was put on trial for spreading this rumour – and the magistrates insisted the case was held in secret to stop the rumour spreading any further. She was lucky – she was only put in prison. The usual punishment for gossip was to have your ears cut off!

In fact it doesn't seem likely that Liz was doing anything with Rob that would get her into trouble. She was surrounded by servants the whole time, and every one of them always swore that Liz was behaving herself. Elizabeth said she was, but she added that even if she wasn't she didn't see who in the country was in a position to tell the Queen what to do.

This didn't stop the suitors and their ambassadors worrying. (No king or prince wanted to marry a wanton woman in those days.) The Emperor Charles V, father of Archduke Charles, instructed his ambassador to get to the bottom of the rumours. Here's what he wrote:

> *I have employed as my agent a certain Francis Borth, who is on very friendly terms with all the Ladies of the Bedchamber. They all swear by what is holy that Her Majesty has never been forgetful of her honour. Yet it is not without significance that Her Majesty shows her liking for Lord Robert more markedly than is consistent with her reputation and dignity.*

It wasn't just the suitors who didn't like the Queen's love for Rob Dudley. The other courtiers hated him. Thomas Howard, Duke of Norfolk was a special enemy. At one stage, Dudley's followers went round the court wearing purple while Norfolk's wore yellow.

Norfolk was jealous of Dudley, who was always getting presents of land and titles from the Queen. If people wanted Dudley to use his influence with the Queen they had to give him a backhander to do it.

Sir Nicholas Throckmorton, English ambassador in Paris, said: 'I pray for the sake of England, her security and prestige, and Her Majesty's own reputation, that she does not so foully forget herself as to marry Lord Robert Dudley.'

The Queen's old nanny, Kat Ashley didn't like Dudley, and neither did the Queen's chief adviser, William Cecil. Cecil was away negotiating with the Scots as the romance got under way. When he came back he found Dudley was acting as her Chief Adviser. Cecil was worried. It looked as though the Queen would marry her 'bonny sweet Robin' when Amy Dudley died. Then Cecil would be out of a job.

Cecil had a good moan to the Spanish ambassador, Bishop de Quadra, on the 8th September 1560. He told him that:

- Elizabeth was behaving so badly with Dudley that he (Cecil) was going to resign from her service and go and live in the country – if they didn't send him to the Tower first.
- Liz didn't think she needed any of the foreign princes and was just playing games with them.
- Liz and Dudley were plotting to murder Dudley's wife so that they could get married.

THE TUDOR TATLER

9 September 1560

AMY DUDLEY FOUND DEAD

Amy Dudley – wife of the Queen's favourite, Lord Robert – was found dead yesterday at Cumnor Place near Abingdon, her neck broken at the foot of a flight of stairs.

Amy, 28, who has been suffering a disease of the breast, had been depressed recently. On Sunday the Fair of Our Lady was held at Abingdon and Lady Dudley insisted that all the servants go out – leaving her alone in the house with just her companion, Mistress Odingsells, and a Mistress Owen. When the servants returned from the fair, Amy's crumpled body was lying at the foot of a flight of stairs.

'No one is to blame for this. It was just a terrible accident,' said a spokesman for Sir Antony Forster, the treasurer of Lord Dudley's household, who owns Cumnor Place.

The Queen has been told and is said to be speechless with shock. She has put the court into mourning and is keeping to her Privy Chamber. Lord Robert has left her side and is now living alone at his house at Kew, pending a full inquiry into Amy's death.

Privately people were commenting that it is unlikely that Lord Dudley, who was widely tipped as the man most likely to marry the Queen, will now be able to do so.

Whodunnit?

What happened to Amy Dudley? The circumstances were odd. Why was she so keen for everyone to leave the house that afternoon? Why did Cecil, who was normally so careful and discreet, pour out his heart to the Spanish ambassador the same weekend she died? Was she dying? If so, who would want to murder her?

At the time a lot of people thought she had been killed by Robert Dudley. The coroner brought in a verdict of accidental death but ever since the day she died people have been putting forward theories. See which one you think is most likely.

1 She committed suicide because she was ill and depressed by all the rumours about her husband.
FOR: Might account for Amy telling everyone to leave the house – suicide was a mortal sin in those days and nobody ever said you'd committed suicide unless it was unmistakable.
AGAINST: Throwing yourself downstairs isn't a very good way of killing yourself; you might break a few bones and still live on in pain and misery.

2 She died of natural causes after an accidental fall.
FOR: Advanced breast cancer sometimes causes the bones to weaken, so that quite a small fall or shock can cause a broken bone.

111

AGAINST: Doesn't explain why Amy was so keen to be alone in the house that afternoon.

3 She was murdered by her husband (possibly aided and abetted by Liz).
FOR: With Amy out of the way, Rob would be free to marry Liz.
AGAINST: Amy was ill and

would have died soon anyway. A death in mysterious circumstances made marriage with the Queen less likely, not more so.

4 She was murdered by agents of William Cecil.
FOR: Cecil's career looked up with Amy's mysterious death. He soon got his job as Chief Adviser back again. Cecil had behaved very oddly with the Spanish ambassador, spreading nasty rumours about Liz and Rob planning to poison Amy. It's possible that Amy wanted everyone out of the house because she was expecting a messenger from Cecil.
AGAINST: All the evidence is circumstantial; there are no witnesses and no forensic evidence to tie Cecil to this crime.

The fact is, we'll never know what really happened to Amy Dudley. When her coffin was opened in the twentieth century there was nothing in it but dust. We do know Cecil was right back in favour as soon as Dudley was banished to Kew, and for the rest of Dudley's life there was always a question mark over him which ruled him out as Elizabeth's husband.

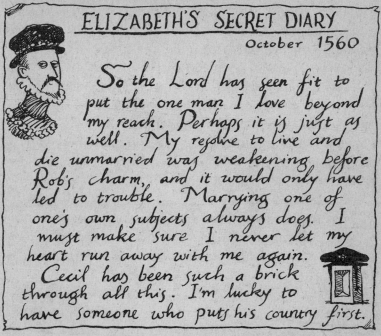

ELIZABETH'S SECRET DIARY

October 1560

So the Lord has seen fit to put the one man I love beyond my reach. Perhaps it is just as well. My resolve to live and die unmarried was weakening before Rob's charm, and it would only have led to trouble. Marrying one of one's own subjects always does. I must make sure I never let my heart run away with me again. Cecil has been such a brick through all this. I'm lucky to have someone who puts his country first.

Robert Dudley was back in the Queen's favour as soon as the coroner said, 'Accidental death'.

OH WELL – ACCIDENTS WILL HAPPEN.

PHEW!

He remained her Master of Horse and they stayed close friends for the rest of their lives. Liz called him 'Sir Eyes'. She didn't want him to marry anyone else, but she was much too wise to mess up her own career by marrying him – or anyone else.

The cult of the Virgin Queen

Having decided marriage was a no-win strategy, Elizabeth decided to make a big thing of staying single. She called herself the Virgin Queen and said she was wedded to the English people. They liked that. She'd made a conquest of people's hearts.

Elizabeth had decided to be a Virgin Queen out of necessity. But she was a mistress of PR, and so she made out – most of the time – that it had always been her strategy. Plus her spin-doctors were probably helped by a prophecy which was supposed to have been made by King Arthur's wizard, Merlin:

> *Then shall a royal virgin reign which shall stretch her white rod over the Belgic shore and the great Castile smite so sore withal that it shall make him shake and fall.*

Castile was Spain ... so watch this space.

Royal progresses

There was nothing Liz liked better than to get out and about during the summer months. It was a good way of seeing the country, and of being seen (and spoken to) by the people. It also kept the housekeeping bills down because Elizabeth and as many of her court that would fit would go and stay in the houses of local bigwigs. Everyone else had to find places to stay nearby. They couldn't stay more than a few days in any one house because there were so many of them that they ate everyone out of house and home.

There was great excitement in the towns and villages when the Royal Progress passed through. Here's a real poem that was written at the time.

No sooner was pronounced the name
But babes in street 'gan leap;
The youth, the aged, the rich, the poor,
Came running all on heap,
And clapping hands and calling out,
'O blessed be the hour!
Our queen is coming to the town
With princely train and power.'

Royal Progresses brought a lot of trade to the towns, but they were a real headache for Elizabeth's security chiefs. The Queen stopped and spoke to anyone she wanted to, and broke lots of other security rules.

Here's what the citizens of Sandwich in Kent had to say about preparations for the Queen's visit in 1565.

WHAT A CLEANING THE TOWN THERE HAS BEEN THIS PAST MONTH. THE STREETS ALL SWEPT OF DIRT, THE HOUSES BEDECKED WITH FLAGS AND TAPESTRIES, HER WAY STREWN WITH RUSHES AND PETALS.

FULL ONE HUNDRED AND SIXTY DISHES DID WE PREPARE, ROAST VENISON AND PIGEON AND BLACKBIRD PIE, ROAST BEEF, AND THEN BLANCMANGE AND SWEETMEATS AND BAKED CUSTARDS. TRULY I NEVER SAW SO MUCH FOOD!

THE QUEEN ARRIVED, RIDING A PALFREY, WITH ROBERT DUDLEY, MASTER OF HORSE, BESIDE HER. SO REGAL SHE WAS, AND YET RELAXED WITH IT. ANY MAN MIGHT APPROACH AND SPEAK TO HER, AND MANY DID.

FIRST SHE HEARD THE CHILDREN OF THE TOWN SING AND THEN DID SHE WATCH OUR PAGEANT WHICH WE HAD LONG PRACTISED AND REHEARSED, AND SHE SAID SHE WAS WELL PLEASED WITH IT !

SHE SAT HERSELF DOWN AT OUR TRESTLE AND WITHOUT ANY TASTING SHE SAMPLED SOME HALF-DOZEN DISHES AND PRONOUNCED HERSELF AMAZED AT THE TASTES AND SMELLS AND PLENTY WE HAD SET BEFORE HER.

TRULY, AND I DO NOT BELIEVE THERE IS ANOTHER TOWN IN THE COUNTRY WHICH BOASTS SUCH GREAT COOKS AMONG ITS HOUSEWIVES AS THIS FAIR TOWN OF SANDWICH IN KENT.

THERE IS SO MUCH MORE I COULD TELL YOU — HER FINE DRESS, ENCRUSTED WITH JEWELS, HER CLOAK, HER FINE HANDS, HER EYES WHICH MISS NOTHING AND SEEM TO KNOW EVERYTHING...

THOUGH SHE BE NOT SO MUCH BIGGER THAN OTHER FOLK, SHE DO *SEEM* BIGGER AND BRIGHTER AND MORE REAL. TRULY WE ARE LUCKY TO HAVE SUCH A GREAT QUEEN WHO PAYS SUCH ATTENTION TO HER SUBJECTS.

It was unusual for the Queen to eat food outside the palace and unheard of for her to eat it without someone else sampling it first, in case it had been poisoned. But Liz tucked in at Sandwich, while her security chiefs crossed their fingers and held their breath. And the citizens of Sandwich were delighted. So was Liz. She had won their hearts. It was yet another successful PR exercise – another conquest.

But not everyone was so thrilled to know she was coming.

It cost a fortune to feed the court and it was also expected that her hosts (usually the richest noblemen in the area) would give her expensive presents as well. In one house she received a diamond pendant, a pair of virginals, a new frock, and still she asked for a fancy saltcellar, and a knife and spoon as she left.

LIZZY'S WORLD: The Queen's Palaces

Elizabeth owned 60 castles and houses as well as about a dozen palaces. Many of the best palaces were on the river. Liz used to travel between them by barge, while her luggage followed by road.

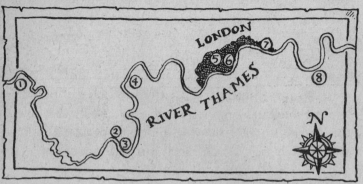

1 Windsor Castle Difficult to heat, so Liz only came in summer. She built a stone terrace outside her apartments so she could get some fresh air and exercise, and another long gallery inside the house where she marched up and down in wet weather. At Windsor Castle there were bathrooms with running water and the Queen loved to hunt in the Great Park.

2 Nonsuch Near Hampton Court in Surrey, this was one of Liz's favourite palaces. It had been built by her father with white and gold towers at all four corners. When Liz was in residence there were tents everywhere, because there wasn't enough room for all the courtiers.

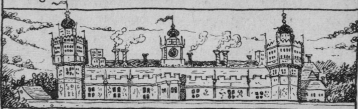

3 Hampton Court Liz nearly died of smallpox here in 1562, so she wasn't mad about this palace. The walls were all beautifully carved and painted with gold and silver.

4 Richmond Palace Loads of domes and turrets, a pinnacle, and wonderful gardens. Pure spring water was pumped into the palace, and there were 18 kitchens. The most draught-proof of the royal palaces, Liz called it her 'nest for old age'.

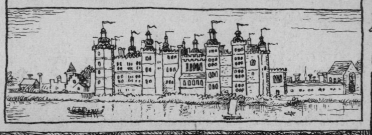

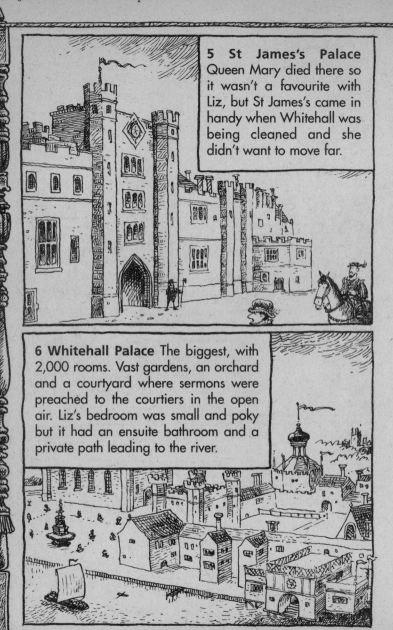

5 St James's Palace
Queen Mary died there so it wasn't a favourite with Liz, but St James's came in handy when Whitehall was being cleaned and she didn't want to move far.

6 Whitehall Palace The biggest, with 2,000 rooms. Vast gardens, an orchard and a courtyard where sermons were preached to the courtiers in the open air. Liz's bedroom was small and poky but it had an ensuite bathroom and a private path leading to the river.

7 The Tower of London Still there today. Liz hated it. She never stayed there after her coronation. The Crown Jewels lived there and Liz's ceremonial robes, while the royal apartments were always kept ready just in case she showed up. In Liz's day there was also a mini-zoo.

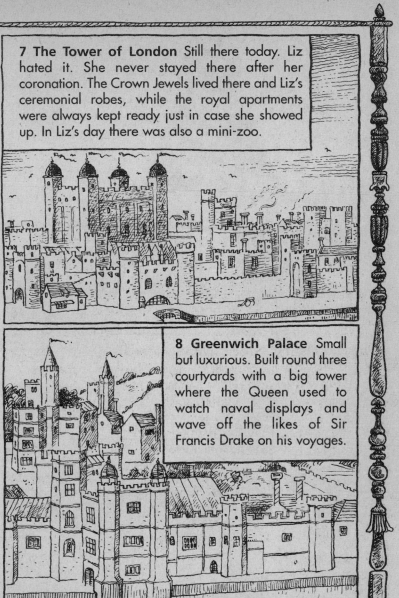

8 Greenwich Palace Small but luxurious. Built round three courtyards with a big tower where the Queen used to watch naval displays and wave off the likes of Sir Francis Drake on his voyages.

123

PESKY COUSIN MARY

Elizabeth was doing quite well during the first few years of her reign. She was managing to hold the middle ground between the Catholics and the extreme Protestants. She was managing to put off marriage and making a big PR success out of being England's Virgin Queen. Plus she didn't have to worry about a half-sister of the opposite religion waiting in the wings for her to die (unlike Edward VII and Mary I). But she did have a pesky cousin, who would be a serious threat throughout her life, Mary Queen of Scots.

Mary Stewart and Liz both had Henry VII for a grandad. Mary's dad, Scots king James V, had died when she was a week old. Her mum, Marie of Guise, came from one of the most powerful families in France. She sent Mary to France when she was six, while she herself stayed behind to rule Scotland (or try to). By the age of 14, Mary was married to the French Dauphin, or Crown-Prince. And when Mary Tudor died, Mary Queen of Scots' father-in-law, the French king, saw his chance and stepped in to announced that Mary Stewart was the rightful Queen of England.

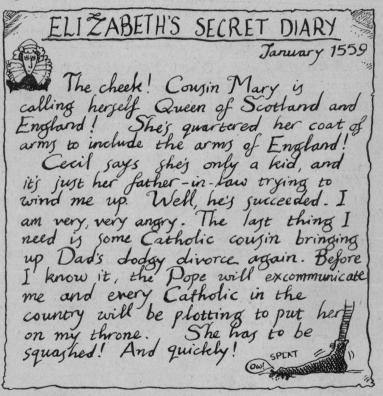

ELIZABETH'S SECRET DIARY

January 1559

The cheek! Cousin Mary is calling herself Queen of Scotland and England! She's quartered her coat of arms to include the arms of England! Cecil says she's only a kid, and it's just her father-in-law trying to wind me up. Well, he's succeeded. I am very, very angry. The last thing I need is some Catholic cousin bringing up Dad's dodgy divorce again. Before I know it, the Pope will excommunicate me and every Catholic in the country will be plotting to put her on my throne. She has to be squashed! And quickly!

OW! SPLAT

Liz was worried England was now jammed between two enemies, France and French Scotland.

Fortunately for Liz, a fiery Scottish preacher called John Knox was leading a Protestant revolution in Scotland. Elizabeth couldn't stand John Knox, but she was delighted that so many Scottish nobles were anti-French and anti-Catholic. They wanted England to help them in their fight to get rid of the French.

Liz had learned two lessons in her stormy childhood:

1) Say nothing; keep them guessing.

2) Lie through your teeth.

This time she went for option two. She sent money to help the Scots, but secretly.

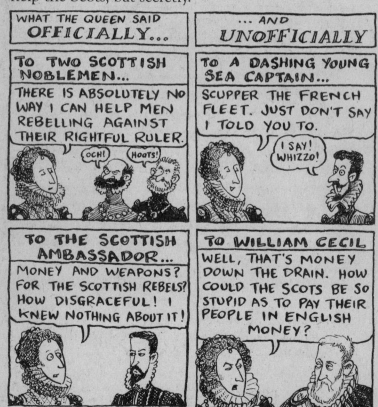

Cecil was keen to invade Scotland and support the Scottish rebels, but Elizabeth was much too canny. She thought war was a waste of men and money. Besides, the Protestant lords weren't doing very well, and the Spanish might join in on the side of the French. So she sent Cecil up to Scotland to talk to the Regent, Marie of Guise, who was desperate for some sort of settlement with the Scottish nobles. He came back with the Treaty of Edinburgh.

The Treaty of Edinburgh

1. Henceforth, in the interests of peace in Scotland, the government of Scotland shall be in the hands of a council of Scottish nobles.
2. All French troops are to be withdrawn from Scotland forthwith.
3. Mary Queen of Scots and her husband, King Francis II of France, agree that Elizabeth is the rightful Queen of England. They agree henceforth to desist from calling Mary Queen of England; they further agree that Mary will stop using the crest of England on her coat-of-arms.

Signed this 6th day of July 1560

William Cecil
(for H M Queen Elizabeth of England)

William Maitland
(for the Dowager Queen and Regent of Scotland, Marie de Guise)

This treaty was great news for Liz and it brought peace to Scotland. Cecil came back to London, expecting to be praised and rewarded. This was around the time when Liz was wild about Rob Dudley – and not long before his wife's death.

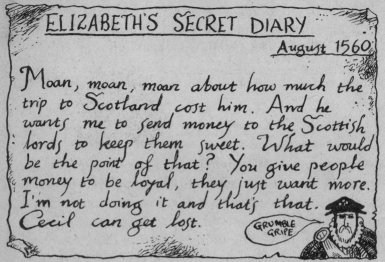

ELIZABETH'S SECRET DIARY

August 1560

Moan, moan, moan about how much the trip to Scotland cost him. And he wants me to send money to the Scottish lords to keep them sweet. What would be the point of that? You give people money to be loyal, they just want more. I'm not doing it and that's that. Cecil can get lost.

GRUMBLE GRIPE

Cecil never did get rewarded for the money he had spent on negotiating the deal with Scotland. But with Dudley tainted by his wife's mysterious death, Cecil was back at the Queen's side. Scotland was at peace; the only trouble was that Mary Queen of Scots and her husband, the French king, refused to sign the Treaty of Edinburgh. In other words...

I'M STILL QUEEN OF ENGLAND!

Then suddenly, in December 1560, the young French king died of an ear infection. Mary Queen of Scots was a widow at 19. She decided to go and live in Scotland. She sent a message to Elizabeth, asking if it was OK if she travelled via England. Liz saw her chance.

> NOT UNLESS YOU SIGN THE TREATY OF EDINBURGH.

Mary didn't sign. She didn't travel via England either. She went by sea to Scotland, where her half-brother, James Moray, had taken over the government since her mother's death. She was in for a tough time, because Scotland was becoming more and more Protestant and Mary was a Catholic. But she was young and charming, and at first all her subjects were happy to have their glam young queen in their midst.

Now she had no husband, Mary wanted to be friends with Elizabeth. She knew Liz wanted her to sign the Treaty of Edinburgh. She said she would if Liz recognized her as heir to the throne of England. Liz wasn't keen.

> OH NO! I KNOW HOW KEEN MEN WERE TO PUT ME ON MY SISTER'S THRONE WHEN I WAS HEIR...

Royal competition

Liz was scared that Mary would be a magnet for the Catholic rebels in her kingdom, the way Liz had been a magnet for Protestants in her sister's time. And she was also jealous of Mary, who had knocked her off her perch as Best Catch in Europe.

BEST CATCH IN EUROPE COMPETITION

ELIZABETH

- QUEEN OF ENGLAND.
- YOUNG, CLEVER, BOSSY.
- FLIRTS OUTRAGEOUSLY WITH MAN SUSPECTED OF MURDER.
- KEEPS PUTTING OFF SUITORS.

MARY

- QUEEN OF SCOTLAND.
- LIKELY TO BE QUEEN OF ENGLAND ONE DAY.
- POWERFUL GUISE FAMILY BEHIND HER.
- YOUNG, FEMININE, BEAUTIFUL.
- KEEN TO FIND A HUSBAND.

The Scottish ambassador to the English court was Sir James Melville. Lizzy was always showing off in front of him. She wanted him to think she was much better than Mary. Not only that … she wanted him to *tell* her so.

One evening, after Melville had told her that Mary played the virginals, she made sure he 'accidentally' came into a room where she just happened to be playing the virginals herself. Melville had got her number by now. He knew you could never pay Elizabeth enough compliments. He said that as he walked by...

> I heard such music as ravished me and drew me within the chamber.

Liz was delighted, but it didn't stop her next question. Can you guess what it was?

ELIZABETH'S SECRET DIARY

September 1564

I am sick of hearing how beautiful she is! How graceful! How beautifully she dances! How agreeable! It's like pulling teeth getting my courtiers to tell me I'm beautiful, but Mary has them all drooling.

I shall have to watch out who she marries. Philip's out of the picture, thank goodness, since he married Elisabeth of France. But I don't want her married to Charles or Ferdinand, she'd be much too powerful.

One of my people, that's who she should marry. And I know the very man.

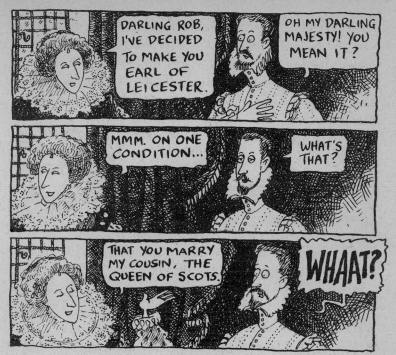

Dudley was horrified at the idea of being sent to Scotland. He looked thoroughly gloomy when the Queen knighted him. And she shocked everyone by tickling his neck in the middle of the solemn ceremony. He needn't have worried. Mary didn't want a man with rumours of murder hanging over him. Besides, she had fallen in love.

The man of her dreams was Henry Darnley, son of the Countess of Lennox. Darnley was an Englishman with a claim to the English throne, and he should have got

Elizabeth's permission to marry, because any children he had with Mary would have a strong claim to the English throne. When Liz heard that Darnley and Mary were married without her permission, she was outraged. She sent Darnley's mum, the Countess of Lennox, straight to the Tower.

WELL THAT SEEMS A BIT UNFAIR...

Despite her anger, Elizabeth was now back as Best Catch in Europe again. And she was about to see unfold in front of her eyes what might have happened if she'd followed her heart and married hunky Rob Dudley.

Mary's disastrous marriages

Lord Darnley was younger than Mary and very spoilt. He drank a lot, and he was always taking off with other women. He also got it into his head that she was two-timing him with her Italian secretary, David Rizzio. A bunch of nobles roped him into a plot to kill Rizzio.

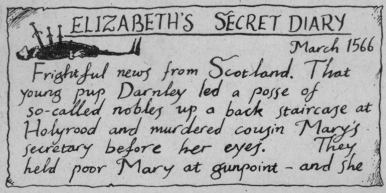

ELIZABETH'S SECRET DIARY

March 1566

Frightful news from Scotland. That young pup Darnley led a posse of so-called nobles up a back staircase at Holyrood and murdered cousin Mary's secretary before her eyes. They held poor Mary at gunpoint – and she seven months pregnant. It's a wonder she didn't lose the baby.

I can't make head or tail of what happened next. It seems she and Darnley rode through the night to Dunbar castle. Which means she must be condoning the murder!

Not long afterwards, Mary gave birth to a son.

ELIZABETH'S SECRET DIARY

24th June 1566

Sir James Melville arrived while we were dancing this Sunday eve. I saw him speaking with Cecil out of the corner of my eye. Then Cecil came over to speak to me. He brought news of cousin Mary who gave birth to a healthy son four days ago. She and cousin Darnley have called him James. If he lives he will be the sixth king of that name in Scotland. And if I remain child-less, who knows, one day he may be the first James to rule over my own realm of England. When I am gone, that is. Till then I am Queen.

Cousin Mary wishes me to be his godmother. I have agreed, and sent Sir James back to Scotland with a gold font, studded with gems. A present for the child.

Three months later there was more dramatic news from Scotland. Darnley was dead. There had been an explosion at the house where he was living. The main suspect was the rough, tough Earl of Bothwell – and Mary was letting him get away with it. Four months later, the news came that Mary had married Bothwell!

Elizabeth knew what a terrible effect this would have on Mary's reputation. Here's an extract from the real letter she wrote to her:

No good friend you have in the world can like thereof, and if we should otherwise write or say, we should abuse you. For how can a worse choice be made for your honour than in such haste to marry such a subject who, besides other notorious lacks, public fame has charged with the murder of your husband?

Liz was right. Mary, top of the pops when she arrived in Scotland, was now bottom of the charts with her subjects. In the civil war that followed, Mary was defeated. Instead of going to France, where she had friends and family, Mary decided to go to England, where she knew no one. It was an incredibly stupid decision.

The last thing Elizabeth needed was a Catholic cousin with a claim to the English throne gate-crashing her country. So it wasn't exactly surprising that Mary found herself a Guest of Her Majesty for the next 19 years.

Poor old Mary had no idea this was what would happen.

> 18th May 1568
>
> Dearest cousin,
> I know you will be as shocked as me by the way my subjects have treated me. It is for this reason that I have thrown myself on your mercy. I beg you to send an army and restore me to my rightful throne.
> Your dearest cousin... and, dare I say, heir?
> Mary (still Queen of Scots whatever anyone says)

Rather surprisingly Liz was all for helping Mary at first. Maybe it was just to get rid of her. Maybe not. It was one of her most basic beliefs that kings and queens were sent by God to rule their subjects, and that subjects had no right to kick them out.

Elizabeth's councillors didn't agree. They said Mary was probably guilty of Darnley's murder and that Liz should hand her cousin over to Mary's half-brother Lord James Moray, who was ruling Scotland with a Protestant coalition.

In the end it was decided to hold an inquiry. The inquiry said Lord James Moray hadn't proved Mary was guilty of murder, but Mary hadn't proved she was innocent either. But while James Moray went home to Scotland with £5,000, Mary was shut up in Tutbury Castle, a prisoner of the Queen of England.

A dangerous prisoner

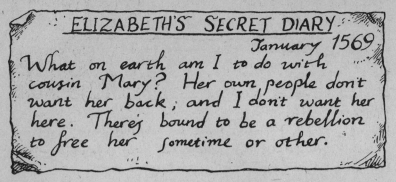

ELIZABETH'S SECRET DIARY

January 1569

What on earth am I to do with cousin Mary? Her own people don't want her back; and I don't want her here. There's bound to be a rebellion to free her sometime or other.

Liz was absolutely right. Quite soon there was a rebellion of the northern Catholic dukes and earls, who marched south planning to liberate Mary and make her Queen of England. (It failed.) About the same time, the Pope got all excited about the prospect of a Catholic queen, and excommunicated Elizabeth.

Parliament and council were outraged. They urged Liz to clamp down on Catholics. From then on it cost you:

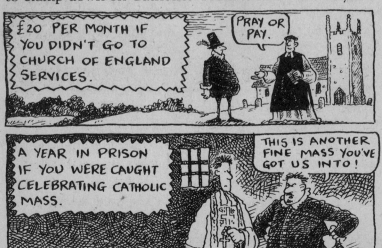

It was the beginning of the end of Liz's even-handed religious policy. From then on, Elizabeth was hard on Catholics – though nothing like as hard as her sister had been on Protestants.

Meanwhile, Mary continued to plot against Liz at every opportunity. Mary's great talent was for making men fall in love with her. The Duke of Norfolk had fallen for her when he was chairing the inquiry.

Elizabeth put him in the Tower because he was getting ideas about marrying her. When she let him out, he was plotting with an Italian banker called Ridolfi and the Spanish Duke of Alva within weeks. He was arrested again, and this time he was tried for treason and sentenced to death. At first Liz refused to sign the warrant for his execution. She hated executing people, especially those she knew well.

ELIZABETH'S SECRET DIARY

31st May 1572

Cecil and Dudley are both on at me all the time to execute Mary. I know she is a danger to me and I can never restore her to her kingdom, but I will not kill her. (Though I wish someone else would.) She is my cousin, but more important, she has powerful allies. All those Guise uncles in France — I don't want them coming down on me like a ton of bricks.

I have, however, signed the warrant for Norfolk's execution. I have to. I must show people what happens to any who plot with her against me and my kingdom. But I hate doing it. He's such a nice young man.

The Duke of Norfolk was beheaded on 2nd June 1572. Elizabeth had been on the throne for fourteen years.

I HAVE NEVER BEEN A PAPIST, BUT THE SENTENCE IS JUST. SINCE THE BEGINNING OF OUR GRACIOUS QUEEN'S REIGN, I AM THE FIRST TO SUFFER DEATH IN THIS PLACE, AND GOD GRANT I MAY BE THE LAST.

LIZZY'S WORLD: The Queen's Ladies.

SITUATIONS VACANT

A rare opportunity to work in the best household in the land. Due to the death of one of the Queen's ladies-in-waiting, a vacancy has arisen for a maid of honour.

Applicants should be between the ages of 14 and 25; be of English birth; should speak Latin, Greek, and either French, Italian or Spanish in addition to English. A talent for music and a love of philosophy and outdoor pursuits would be an advantage.

Please write, giving full particulars of birth and parentage to the following address.
Box number TT 1212.

Rich families paid good money to have their daughters taken on at court. Whenever there was a vacancy, lots of families rushed to try and get their daughters a job.

The Queen had loads of ladies-in-waiting:

SEVEN LADIES OF THE BEDCHAMBER (WHO LOOKED AFTER HER IN THE WITHDRAWING ROOM; ONE DUTY WAS TO READ ALOUD TO HER).

BLAH...

SIX MAIDS OF HONOUR (WHO RAN ERRANDS, CARRIED HER TRAIN, LOOKED AFTER HER CLOTHES, SCATTERED FLOWER PETALS IN FRONT OF HER AS SHE WALKED).

STREW

FOUR CHAMBERERS (WHO TIDIED UP AFTER HER).

EWW...

Elizabeth insisted her ladies-in-waiting wore black and white, the way she had as a young girl. This was so she herself stood out more in her bright colours and jewels. Once, when she thought a lady-in-waiting was putting her in the shade with a brightly-coloured dress, she secretly tried on her dress. It didn't fit, so Liz told the woman she wasn't to wear it any more as it was too good for her!

Liz also had a reputation for being a real tartar with her ladies and not wanting them to get married. Here are some ladies – and gents – who fell foul of the Queen.

Lady Katherine Grey
Sister of Jane. She would have had the best Protestant claim to the throne, except she'd become a Catholic under Mary. Elizabeth knew the Spanish were keen to marry her off to one of their princes, so she made her a Lady of the Bedchamber so she could keep an eye on her.

But young Kath was in love with Edward Seymour, son of the old Lord Protector. They married secretly, helped by Edward's sister, Jane. Katherine went back to court and by the time she went on a Royal Progress with Liz, people were giving her funny looks because she was pregnant.

Liz was outraged. She put Katherine and Edward in the Tower (in separate cells).

Kath gave birth to a baby boy with a *very* good claim to the throne. And there was no stopping Kath and

Ed! Despite being in the Tower, Katherine had another child a year later!

Liz had her lawyers examine the legality of the marriage. They were unable to find the priest, and with no witness (sister Jane had died in the meantime) they declared the marriage invalid. That meant the boys were illegitimate, which dented their claim to the throne. As for poor old Kath, she was kept in the Tower for seven years until her death in 1568.

Lady Mary Grey
Jane's younger sister, who had a deformed back and was very tiny, fell for a giant commoner called Thomas Keyes. He was the Queen's Serjeant-Porter (which meant he did a lot of fetch and carry) and he and Mary married secretly. There was no real danger that they would produce a possible heir to the crown, but Liz did her nut again. Keyes was sent to the Fleet prison for three years, Mary was put under house arrest, and Liz tried to have this marriage declared invalid too (she failed). In the end she let Keyes out of prison on condition he vowed never to see Mary again and when Keyes died she refused to let Mary wear black for him.

Lady Mary Shelton

When this lady-in-waiting secretly married Sir James Scudamore, the Queen was 'liberal with her blows'. Mary came out of the meeting with a broken finger. Elizabeth later apologized and promoted Mary to Lady of the Privy Chamber.

Lady Anne Vavasour

She didn't bother with a ceremony and ended up with an illegitimate child. She was sent away from court in disgrace – but Liz did make the father cough up £2,000 for the child.

Lady Mary Fitton

She dressed up as a man to go out and meet her feller, and was banished from court forever.

Does all this make Liz sound like a complete lunatic? If so, it's not quite true. It was only when the marriage might mean the birth of an heir to the

145

throne, or when she wanted the man for herself, that she really went incandescent. The rest of the time she was just like a bossy headmistress (and some of 'her girls' were very young, and her courtiers very wild). She wanted them to behave well so they were a credit to the court.

Many of the Queen's ladies stayed with her all her life. They were her best friends.

- Blanche Parry (Thomas's wife) and Kat Ashley, her servants from childhood, stayed with her till they died.
- So did Lady Mary Sidney, who was a real brainbox, and mother of the poet Sir Philip Sidney.
- Lady Mary Radcliffe refused to get married at all just so she could be like the Queen. No doubt Liz wished all her courtiers were more like Mary.

MONEY AND MEN

It may be thought simplicity in me that all this time of my reign I have not sought to advance my territories and enlarge my dominions, for opportunity hath served me to do it. My mind was never to invade my neighbours or usurp over any. I am contented to rule over mine own and to rule as a just prince.

Although she made many conquests, Elizabeth never conquered other countries. This wasn't because she was very saintly. She couldn't afford it and she realized it. Compared with the French and Spanish kings, Liz was hard up.

I CAN'T AFFORD TO GET IN TROUBLE...

ELIZABETH'S ACCOUNT BOOK.

INCOME	OUTGOINGS
Rents from Crown land : £130,000	Court expenses inc. housekeeping: £70,000
Customs and Excise : £90,000	Govt. ministers' salaries: £20,000
	Dress allowance: £30,000
	Interest on debts: £100,000
TOTAL: £220,000	TOTAL: £220,000

It was a miracle of money-management that Elizabeth managed to get her costs down so low. Out of her income of £220,000 she had to run the court, pay her councillors, and run the country.

War was the only thing she could ask Parliament to raise taxes for. Liz knew her subjects didn't like taxes, that's why she stayed away from war. The only other way she could raise money was by taking out loans from moneylenders in Antwerp in the Netherlands. If she failed to pay back the loan, the moneylenders could nab the goods of any English merchants. That wouldn't have been very popular either. So Liz scrimped and saved and refused to bail out her councillors or bribe her allies to stick by her. And, above all, she tried to avoid war.

However, Liz didn't mind a bit of skirmishing with the enemy provided she didn't know about it and it didn't cost her anything. And it so happened that there were a number of jack-the-lad sea captains around who enjoyed making fools of the Spanish. Liz got on well with these guys, who were mainly Protestant, loyal to her, and always up for an adventure. The most famous of them was Francis Drake.

Drake's voyages

1572 Drake captures a huge haul of gold and jewels which the Spanish had discovered in the New World and brings it back to England. Liz invites him to meet her and wants to know all about his travels.

1577 Liz is so chuffed with Drake that she goes into business with him and invests lots of money in his latest expedition to the New World. Walsingham, Leicester and Sir Christopher Hatton are also investors. Drake sets off on a round the world voyage.

1580 Drake arrives home with £800,000 of stolen treasure, not to mention some sample potatoes and tobacco plant, and tales of strange creatures called llamas.

It wasn't surprising Elizabeth was so pleased with Drake – £160,000 of the £800,000 Spanish treasure was her return on her investment. (In fact you could say that this captured treasure had been stolen by the Spanish in the first place, since Spain was taking it from mines and ancient Indian tombs in South America.)

Drake also gave her a magnificent crown with five emeralds which she wore the following New Year's Day. Liz's account books looked pretty healthy that year.

It proved easier to grow potatoes than tobacco in England. The tobacco needed a warmer climate. One of Elizabeth's chefs got the sack when he cooked the potato leaves instead of the tubers.

The new French suitor

As Philip of Spain got more and more narked with Liz, she realized it might be a good idea to get herself a powerful ally. A French prince would do. The Duke of Anjou, younger brother of the French king, had fallen in love with someone else, but there was a still younger brother...

ELIZABETH'S SECRET DIARY

December 1571

Anjou is out of the picture. Besotted with a Mademoiselle de Chateauneuf, if you please. But I'm told his younger brother,

the Duke of Alençon, is on offer. Only
seventeen, short and covered in pock-marks.
Does not sound promising, though Smith says
he is known to be 'vigorous and lusty'. So
he might get me with child, and that
would put an end to the Scottish
Queen and her claim to the throne.

Zut Alors!

← ◀◀ ACTUAL SIZE

Nothing happened for quite some time. Then in 1578,
Alençon sent his most smooth-talking courtier to suck up to
Liz. Jean de Simier was a dodgy character who had just
murdered his brother, but he was a real charmer, and he soon
had the whole court talking about how cosy he was with Liz.

ELIZABETH'S SECRET DIARY
November 1578

I don't know about the Master, but the man
is very tasty. The dream courtier, he
always knows exactly what to say,
and he has given me a jewelled book
from his master, which I carry on a
chain around my waist. I have
nicknamed him Monkey, and tonight
I am giving a ball in his honour, at
which there will be a masque in
which six ladies surrender to six
suitors.

Not everyone was against Simier. William Cecil, Elizabeth's chief councillor, who was now Lord Burghley, was very keen on a French marriage and an heir who would see off Mary Queen of Scots. Robert Dudley, Earl of Leicester, on the other hand, was very gloomy at the thought of the Queen marrying. However, Simier knew a thing or two about Leicester.

ELIZABETH'S SECRET DIARY

July 1579

Eyes is married. How dare he? He knows that I don't care about any of these foreign suitors. That I have to pretend to like them in order to keep their governments on our side.

I will put him in the Tower, and his beanpole wife. That will teach him. How dare he marry without even telling me? I wanted to marry him.

Liz's councillors pointed out that it wasn't against the law for an unmarried man to marry. Leicester was saved from the Tower, although he was told to stay at home for a bit. When Lettice Dudley showed up at court in her best gear, Liz boxed her ears and said, 'As but one sun lights the East, I will have but one queen in England.' She never had a good word to say for Lettice and called her 'the she-wolf'.

ELIZABETH'S SECRET DIARY

August 1579

I would like to kill Lettice. I hate her. How dare she steal my favourite from right under my nose?

As for Leicester, I'll show him. I'll make him jealous. You just watch.

Maybe Liz had thought that Leicester would always be there for her. Maybe losing him meant she was on the rebound. She certainly decided to make a big play now for Alençon. The first step was to see him in person.

Usually princes and dukes refused point-blank to come to England to be looked over like prize ponies, but Alençon wasn't fazed. He sailed up the Thames to Greenwich in August 1579 on a Dead Secret Mission. (This meant nobody was supposed to know he was there.)

Alençon was put to bed for the day to get over his journey, but at sunset Liz stole out of her palace, accompanied by a single lady-in-waiting to meet him in Simier's pavilion near the river.

ELIZABETH'S SECRET DIARY

18th August 1579

What a turn-up for the books! Frankie d'Alençon is quite a dish! OK, so he is no great height, but he is well-built and positively handsome. Dark, swarthy, muscular, a French duke, a witty courtier-what more could a girl want? I have nicknamed him Frog and made sure everybody heard me say that never in my life have I seen a creature more agreeable to me!

For the next twelve days Alençon stayed in England. He and Liz conducted a secret romance, in snatched moments. Everyone was still pretending he wasn't there, so Liz couldn't invite him to the court ball, so she arranged for him to watch it from behind a screen. Unfortunately she was so keen to impress him that she spent the whole evening waving and smiling in his direction and leaping higher and higher in the air during the dancing. All her courtiers had a hard time pretending not to notice.

LEAP

WHAT A LITTLE MOVER!

The councillors were also pretending he wasn't there. According to the Spanish ambassador: 'They deny Alençon is here and in order not to offend the Queen they shut their eyes and avoid going to court… It is said that if she marries before consulting her people she may repent it. Leicester is much put out and all the councillors are disgusted…'

Fortunately for everyone the visit didn't last long. Alençon was called back to France at the end of August when a friend of his was killed in a duel. By the time he reached home he had sent her seven letters. In one he wrote: 'If Your Majesty will consent to marry me, you will restore a languishing life which has existed only for the service of the most perfect goddess of the heavens.'

Elizabeth liked her men to talk to her like this. She was quite taken with Alençon. She wrote a poem about how she felt. (She really did write one – this is it.)

I grieve, yet dare not show my discontent;
I love, and yet am forced to seem to hate,
I dote but dare not what I meant;
I seem stark mute, yet inwardly do prate.
I am and am not; freeze and yet I burn,
Since from my self my other self I turn.
My care is like my shadow in the sun,
Follows me flying, flies when I pursue it,
Stands and lives by me, does what I have done.
O let me live with some more sweet content
Or die and so forget what love e'er meant.

Wedding bell blues

Marriage negotiations were now under way. However, Elizabeth's councillors put their feet down about some of the terms proposed by the French. They weren't prepared to crown Alençon king of England immediately after the coronation, or to give him an income of £60,000 a year. And Parliament just hated the idea of their English queen marrying a Frenchman.

MARRIAGES WITH FOREIGNERS WILL ONLY RESULT IN THE RUIN OF THE COUNTRY.

The idea of marriage to a Catholic Frenchman was also very unpopular with many of Elizabeth's Protestant subjects. A Puritan called John Stubbs wrote a pamphlet with a very snappy title.

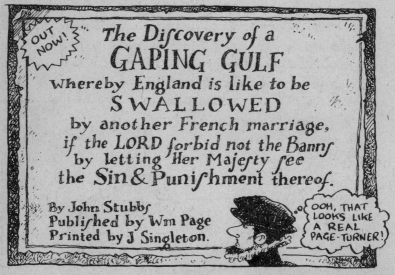

OUT NOW!

The Discovery of a
GAPING GULF
whereby England is like to be
SWALLOWED
by another French marriage,
if the LORD forbid not the Banns
by letting Her Majesty see
the Sin & Punishment thereof.

By John Stubbs
Published by Wm Page
Printed by J Singleton.

OOH, THAT LOOKS LIKE A REAL PAGE-TURNER!

Inside, the pamphlet was very rude about Frankie's family and even suggested to people that they should oppose the Queen. Liz had the screaming abdabs when she read it. She had Stubbs and Page put on trial for inciting people to rebel. She wanted them hanged.

No one could persuade Liz to change her mind. The sentence on Stubbs and Price was carried out, and two judges were sent to gaol.

159

A lot is written about how everyone enjoyed cruelty in Tudor times, but Elizabeth's popularity took a dive at this point. It looked as if Liz's conquest of her people's hearts was well and truly over.

ELIZABETH'S SECRET DIARY

October 1578

Stubbs deserved it. So rude. How dare he insult Frankie and his family. All the same, there is a lot of bad feeling. I am told that as the sentence was carried out the crowd watched silently. With horror.

I had better watch out. I am too like my father when I behave like this. And if I carry on I may not be queen for very long.

But will these people never be satisfied? They are constantly demanding that I marry, and then when I find someone I want to marry, they put all sorts of difficulties in my way.

160

It looks as if Liz really did want to marry Alençon at this stage, but instead of pushing ahead, she asked her councillors what she should do. When they came down against the marriage, she burst into tears. Next day they came back, very contrite, and said that they would do anything if it would make her happy...

ELIZABETH'S SECRET DIARY

November 1578

Darn! They say I can marry him. But I __can't__, because the people are so against it. I have never done anything against the will of my people. What to do?

Liz and Alençon saw each other on and off over the next few years. Alençon was fighting on the Protestant side in the Netherlands and he wanted Lizzy to back him.

On one occasion they appeared together on a balcony and Liz announced that she really was going to marry him. She kissed Alençon on the lips, took a ring from her finger and gave it to him. They were engaged! But then, the very next day, she called him to her Privy Chamber and said she could not marry him, at least not yet.

Eventually she fell out of love, and by the end she wanted rid of him so badly that she paid him £10,000 to go away. Leicester was sent to escort him to Holland, with a secret letter from Elizabeth to William of Orange.

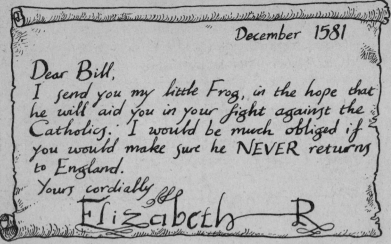

December 1581

Dear Bill,

I send you my little Frog, in the hope that he will aid you in your fight against the Catholics. I would be much obliged if you would make sure he NEVER returns to England.

Yours cordially

Elizabeth R

Some people reported that the Queen did a little dance of triumph when she finally shipped Alençon off to Holland; others said that she went on wearing his jewels and kissing the gloves he had given her. By this time she had really perfected the art of keeping everyone guessing.

When Alençon died a couple of years later Elizabeth went into mourning along with the whole English court. The Queen received John Stubbs at court in 1581. Later on he became an MP.

WELCOME TO PARLIAMENT. LET'S SHAKE HANDS...

ER...

LIZZY'S WORLD: The Court.

The court of Elizabeth was at the heart of government – but it was many other things as well. It was:

- a theatre where the Queen played top of the bill, impressing her foreign visitors with her posh clothes, jewels, furnishings and banquets.

- a club where a lot of networking went on.

- an arts centre, where leading actors, writers, painters and musicians could show off their work.

ARTS PROGRAMME:

Tonight: HENRY IV (Part II), by WILLIAM SHAKESPEARE.

Tomorrow: the latest works by top musician THOMAS TALLIS.

Thursday: EDMUND SPENSER reads from his poem THE FAERIE QUEEN, featuring Elizabeth Tudor as Gloriana, Belphoebe, Judith and other legendary heroines.

Masques and plays were performed for her wherever she went. Many of the chief courtiers (including the Earl of Leicester) had their own theatre companies. In 1583 Liz formed her very own company, known as the Queen's Men. She also had a number of other entertainers on her payroll. These included:

Sometimes the most famous playwrights of her time were invited to put plays on at court. *The Merry Wives of Windsor* was a favourite play of the Queen's. Shakespeare wrote it in two weeks at her special request.

All in all, Elizabeth's court was a lot of fun. The Queen loved everything from dancing to bear-baiting. One minute she was discussing philosophy, the next she was roaring with laughter at her clowns. Or enjoying the tales of her sea captains.

Though she was not a Catholic, she still loved ritual and ceremony, showy clothes, and beautiful church music. The Chapel Royal choristers were world famous.

The Puritans wanted to ban their sort of church music but Liz wasn't having it. And she started concerts at the Royal Exchange so that poor people could enjoy music free of charge.

All Henry's children were brainy and cultured, but Elizabeth was the most tolerant of the three. If people were loyal to the crown, she didn't care what religion they were. The result was that all the best talent came to court and made England famous, not only in Liz's own time, but right down the centuries.

Elizabeth protected the theatres and musicians from the most extreme Protestants who thought any sort of fun was ungodly. Many of these people criticized the court for being wanton and corrupt. Liz made sure it wasn't, though. She was an old tartar when her ladies and gents went too far. She had high standards for courtly manners and behaviour, and if she had had her way all her ladies and gents would have been virgins like herself.

DEATH THREATS AND SEA BATTLES

Elizabeth was nearly fifty by the time it was finally all over with Alençon. There was now no question of her ever producing a baby who would be heir to the throne of England. The person with the best claim to succeed her was Mary Queen of Scots – who was still stuck in prison.

Mary's arrival in England had destabilized Liz's control of her country. Pope Pius V had excommunicated Elizabeth, just after Mary arrived in England back in 1570, and this meant there were always some Englishmen who felt it was their duty to get rid of Liz from the throne of England. Now the Pope went even further.

There is no doubt that whoever sends that guilty woman out of the world with the pious intention of doing God service, not only does not sin, but gains merit.

It was an open invitation to English Catholics to kill the Queen and put Mary on the throne.

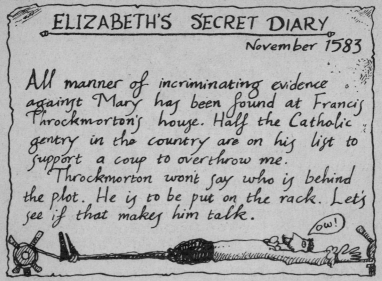

ELIZABETH'S SECRET DIARY

November 1583

All manner of incriminating evidence against Mary has been found at Francis Throckmorton's house. Half the Catholic gentry in the country are on his list to support a coup to overthrow me.

Throckmorton won't say who is behind the plot. He is to be put on the rack. Let's see if that makes him talk.

ow!

The rack was a terrible form of torture which left victims crippled for life. Throckmorton gave nothing away first time round, but the thought of a second session on the rack was too much for him and he told Walsingham (head of Elizabeth's Secret Service) everything he wanted to know. This was how Liz learned that Philip II of Spain (the same Philip who had been married to her sister) was planning 'The Enterprise of England' – a Catholic crusade to conquer England and put Mary Queen of Scots on the English throne.

Throckmorton was hanged at Tyburn and the Spanish ambassador kicked out, but Elizabeth's Parliament and Council were seriously worried by the Throckmorton plot. They thought that Mary Queen of Scots should have been among those executed. Liz wouldn't hear of it, though. Perhaps she remembered how she herself had been the centre of every plot going when her sister was queen, whether she liked it or not. Maybe she simply didn't want to create a Catholic martyr. Whatever the reason, even though she was often angry with Mary, she said there was no real proof against her.

Francis Walsingham decided to change all that. He set out to entrap Mary. (It wasn't very difficult – Mary was desperate to get out of prison.) Pretty soon he had proof that Mary was in league with all sorts of people. The expelled Spanish ambassador was one of them. The French ambassador was another.

> MONSIEUR AMBASSADOR, YOU HAVE MUCH SECRET COMMUNICATION WITH THE QUEEN OF SCOTLAND, BUT BELIEVE ME, I KNOW ALL THAT GOES ON IN MY KINGDOM. I MYSELF WAS A PRISONER IN THE DAYS OF THE OLD QUEEN MY SISTER, AND AM AWARE OF THE TRICKS THAT PRISONERS USE TO WIN OVER SERVANTS AND OBTAIN SECRET INTELLIGENCE.

> OOPS...

Even though Elizabeth told him she was on to him, the French ambassador was so cocky he took no notice. He was in league with various English Catholics, including an eager young man called Sir Anthony Babington. Babington was so confident that his plot to murder Liz and put Mary on the throne would succeed that he had his portrait painted with his fellow-conspirators.

This made life easy for Walsingham. Babington and his mates were put on trial, found guilty and sentenced to be hanged, drawn and quartered.

Death of a royal rival

Young Babington and his mates died a slow and painful death. The problem for Elizabeth was what to do with Mary? Was there any legal way to get rid of her?

In the end it was decided to put Mary on trial. It was clear that she had been plotting against Elizabeth, and so all she had to fall back on was the fact that no court in England had the right to try the queen of another country.

In English law, every man had the right to be tried by his equals. This meant that if you were an earl or a duke on trial you had the right to a jury of earls and dukes. They were your peers, and this is where the word peer, meaning lord, comes from. This tradition also meant that a monarch could never be tried because: 1) he didn't owe any loyalty to anyone else, so he couldn't commit treason; and 2) he had no peers who could judge him.

Despite the law, Mary was tried by a court full of English peers and councillors, found guilty and sentenced to death. If Liz had had trouble signing death warrants before, it was nothing to what she went through this time.

ELIZABETH'S SECRET DIARY

December 1586

What am I to do? If I let her live there will be more plots and more plots and who knows but one of them may succeed.

Yet I don't want to be the one responsible. She's my cousin. More important, she's a queen – sent by God to rule her country. It is not right for me to kill a fellow queen.

And if I do kill her, France and Spain will have the excuse they're looking for to come down on me like a ton of bricks.

Then there's her son. What will he say if I kill his mother? (Actually I think he'll be as pleased as me to see her out of the way, but he's not going to say that in public.)

Why is there not an Englishman alive who will take the matter into his own hands. Why are there so many willing to kill me and no one willing to kill her? Why do I have to do it?

Her ministers were driven mad by her refusal to sign Mary's death warrant. In the end one of her secretaries, Sir John Davison, slipped the warrant in among a lot of other papers she had to sign, so she could pretend she didn't notice what she was signing. As soon as she'd signed it, he hurried away and handed it to Lord Burghley, who made sure the execution was carried out.

HURRY UP, BEFORE SHE CHANGES HER MIND AGAIN...

When she heard it had happened, Liz hit the roof.

ELIZABETH'S SECRET DIARY

19th February 1587

How dare Davison deliver the death warrant? He knew I didn't want poor Mary to die. He knew I'd only signed it just in case it might be needed one day. Now I'm guilty before God of killing the queen of another kingdom. And it gives Philip just the excuse he wants.

Elizabeth was talking rubbish when she blamed Davison, but she was queen, and Davison was only a secretary, so she could say what she liked. She sacked him and never let him come back to court.

But the Protestants in the country – and even some Catholics – were relieved to hear Mary was dead. When they heard the sentence had finally been carried out, Londoners went wild with joy.

THE TUDOR TATLER

20 February 1587

AXED AT LAST!

Cannons roared and church bells rang out in London yesterday to celebrate the death of Queen Elizabeth's most dangerous enemy – the wicked temptress Mary Queen of Scots.

Her own people had had enough of Mary 19 years ago and kicked her out. Since then, Mary has done nothing but plot with the Queen's enemies, in and out of England.

Time and again Elizabeth refused to have her cousin put to death, but Mary learned nothing. Having lost her own kingdom, she was determined to steal someone else's.

Unable to get on with anyone, even her own son, it seems she has bequeathed her right to the English throne to England's deadly enemy – King Philip of Spain.

The Queen is reported to be deeply upset at Mary's death, but this paper says, 'It was not before time, Ma'am. May all your enemies come to the same gory end. God Save Elizabeth, Queen of England!'

Drake to the rescue

Elizabeth had been absolutely right to worry about a Catholic invasion. Philip of Spain had been plotting to put Mary on the English throne for years. (He was fed up with Drake and other English captains stealing his treasure ships.) Now Mary had been executed, he had a cast-iron excuse to march in, depose Liz and avenge her death. He planned to send an armada (Spanish for 'large fleet') to put the English navy out of action, so that Spanish troops could cross from the Netherlands in other, smaller ships, and conquer England.

Sir Francis Drake decided he wouldn't wait till the Spanish Armada came to England. He set sail with a small, specially picked fleet of English ships.

THE TUDOR TATLER
April 1587

THE DRAGON BREATHES FIRE

The King of Spain saw his beard singed this week by English sea-hero, Francis Drake. Displaying immense bravery, and defying all the rules of sea warfare, Drake sailed his small fleet right into Cadiz harbour and, drums rolling, set fire to thousands of tons of Spanish shipping. Not for nothing is he called El Draque, the fire-breathing Dragon, terror of the Spaniards.

Next, bold Drake sailed round to Lisbon and, when the wind dropped, lay at anchor outside the port. Then he sounded his drum, defying the Spaniards to come out and fight. There were no takers. The Spaniards knew we English had the edge with our long-range cannon. They stayed in the harbour quaking in their boots.

Finally Drake sailed to the Azores where he captured a Spanish treasure ship. By this time the Spanish Admiral was on his trail, but Drake fooled him by sailing home to Plymouth with his booty while the Spanish Admiral spent a week looking for him and his fleet in the seas around the islands.

Drake's action set Philip's preparations back a year. In that time Lizzy – who wanted to avoid full-scale war with Spain as much as ever – was trying to get the Duke of Parma, who was leading the Spanish troops in the Netherlands, to agree to peace. Her advisers, including Lord Howard, Admiral of the Fleet, thought she was mad.

> *15th July 1588*
>
> *Madam,*
>
> *I pray you, awake thoroughly and see the villainous treason around you against Your Majesty and your realm. Draw your forces about you like a mighty prince to defend you. Truly, Madam, if you do so there is no cause to fear. If you do not there will be danger.*
>
> *I remain, Madam, your most loyal Admiral,*
>
> *Howard of Effingham*

Finally Liz was convinced that there was no way to avoid this war. The Armada was on its way.

Drake was playing bowls on Plymouth Hoe when the Armada was sighted off the Lizard Peninsula in Cornwall.

WHAT'S THE RUSH? LET'S FINISH OUR GAME...

Actually, it wasn't that Dra
just knew he couldn't sail for
to wait for the tide to turn.

In fact, the English fleet was almost trapped by stormy weather. The wind was blowing the Spanish towards England and keeping the English ships in port. Once again, Drake was full of daring, and the English fleet sailed out in terrible conditions.

st July. Nippy English ships get out of Plymouth
our. Huge Spanish galleons, more difficult to
vre, try to land on the Isle of Wight. The English
landing, and chase the Spaniards out into the
nel.

27th July. The Armada anchors off Calais, with some storm and cannon damage. Drake sends fire-ships into the anchorage, setting fire to many Spanish galleons.

28th July. Big sea battle. The English drive the Spanish past the Netherlands, where they were hoping to land and ship Parma's troops over to England.

29th July. Gales prevent the capture of the Spanish ships, which are driven north and limp home round the north of Scotland. Many ships are wrecked, hundreds of Spaniards drown, and only half the Armada returns to Spain. Not a single English ship has been lost or taken.

Ready for invasion

Meanwhile, English troops had been gathering at Tilbury in case the Duke of Parma landed from the Netherlands. Liz decided that she would go and meet the men who were going to defend their country. Not everyone thought she should go. They were worried about her safety. What if a Catholic from among the troops were to take a shot at her?

Liz had long since forgiven her old pal, Rob Dudley, Earl of Leicester, for his marriage to Lettice. He was now in command of the troops at Tilbury and Liz wrote to him secretly.

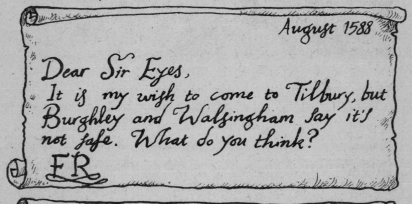

August 1588

Dear Sir Eyes,
It is my wish to come to Tilbury, but Burghley and Walsingham say it's not safe. What do you think?

ER

August 1588

Dear Sweet Queen,
Alter not your purpose. The lodging prepared for Your Majesty is a proper, sweet, cleanly house, the camp within a little mile of it, and your person as sure as at St James's.

I am your most devoted and obedient servant,

Robert Dudley, Earl of Leicester

THE TUDOR TATLER

9 August 1588

ALL THE QUEEN'S MEN

The thousands of troops on standby to repel a Spanish invasion were surprised yesterday by a visit from their queen.

Squadrons of foot soldiers stood to attention. Flags fluttered. Plumed cavalrymen held their horses still as the drummers and pipers played a rousing march.

First came a page carrying the Queen's silver helmet on a white cushion. Then, mounted on a white horse led by the Earl of Leicester, came the Queen herself, dressed in a white velvet dress and a silver breastplate. As she rode up and down the massed ranks of English soldiers, she called out 'God bless you all'. Soon men were calling out 'Lord bless our Queen' and some fell to their knees.

'She looks like an Amazonian empress,' said one nobleman. 'She had tears in her eyes,' said another. 'She looked every man in the face,' said a third. One regiment from Dorset asked if they could buy the honour of guarding the Queen.

Elizabeth was enjoying herself. She loved being out and about among her people, dressed to kill and knowing exactly the right thing to say. Next day she made another conquest with a knockout speech, which left everyone eating out of her hand.

My loving people, we have been persuaded by some that are careful of our safety to take heed how we commit ourselves to armed multitudes, for fear of treachery; but I do assure you that I do not wish to live to distrust my faithful and loving people.

Let tyrants fear. I have always so behaved myself that under God I have placed my chiefest strength and safeguard in the loyal hearts and goodwill of my subjects, and therefore I am come among you, as you see at this time, not for my recreation and disport, but being resolved in the midst and heat of the battle to live or die for my people, my honour and my blood, even i' the dust.

> I know I have the body of a weak and feeble woman, but I have the heart and stomach of a king, and of a king of England too, and think it foul scorn that Parma, or Spain, or any prince of Europe, should dare invade the borders of my realm; to which rather than any dishonour shall grow by me, I myself will take up arms, I myself will be your general, judge and rewarder of every one of your virtues.

(That last bit meant she would pay the troops. Liz had a better record than many rulers on this.)

Next day there were rumours that the Spanish were coming, and Liz, who was getting a bit carried away with her success, said that she was going to lead her men into battle. Fortunately, it was a false alarm. The Duke of Parma bottled out of invading England, and within a week Liz took a chance and disbanded her army before they were sure the danger had passed. (She didn't want to pay the men for a day longer than she really had to.)

The fact was, Elizabeth was right again. The threat of invasion was over. Liz was triumphant. English Catholics did not want a Spanish king ruling them any more than Protestants did. People still remembered the terrible days when Philip had been married to Mary Tudor.

Preparations were made for a great victory celebration, but Liz had something else on her mind.

ELIZABETH'S SECRET DIARY

26th August 1588

Poor Eyes is not well. Terrible stomach pains. This war has been too much for him. I have sent him to the springs at Buxton, to take the waters. I wish to reward him handsomely for his work at Tilbury, but Burghley and Walsingham think it will go to his head.

29th August 1588

I most humbly beseech Your Majesty to pardon your old servant to be thus bold in sending to know how my gracious lady doth. For my own poor case, I continue still your medicine, and it amends much better than any other thing that hath been given me. Thus hoping to find a perfect cure at the bath, with the continuance of my wonted prayer for Your Majesty's most happy preservation, I humbly kiss your foot.

Your Majesty's most faithful and obedient servant,

Robert Dudley, Earl of Leicester

The Earl of Leicester died on 4th of September. Elizabeth was devastated by the news. A Spanish agent told Mendoza:

> SHE WAS SO GRIEVED THAT FOR SOME DAYS SHE SHUT HERSELF IN HER CHAMBER ALONE AND REFUSED TO SPEAK TO ANYONE UNTIL THE TREASURER AND OTHER COUNCILLORS HAD THE DOOR BROKEN OPEN AND ENTERED TO SEE HER.

It didn't make her any more sympathetic to poor old Lettice, Leicester's widow. Leicester had died owing the Queen a lot of money, and Liz wanted it back. She made Lettice auction her furniture to pay the debt, as well as taking back a house that she had given him.

All this, despite the fact that Leicester had left Elizabeth a spectacular necklace of 600 pearls to add to her vast collection of jewels. She wore it for the portrait that was painted to celebrate the English victory over the Armada.

> AND MAKE SURE YOU GET THEM ALL IN.

Her heart wasn't really in the celebrations. She had loved Leicester, even though she had never married him. Now she had lost her best friend.

LIZZY'S WORLD: Fashion Victim?

All the hundreds of portraits of Elizabeth show her wearing heavy brocade dresses covered in jewels with stiff ruffs and wide skirts. This was what she wore for work. Her job was to look super-rich, grand, and stately, and make everyone think England was a fantastic country because they had such a well-dressed queen.

She didn't dress like that all the time. When she was lounging about in her Privy Chamber after her late breakfast she would wear a loose shift (with fur wraps if it was winter). Or she would wear a simple black dress for days at a time. But when it was time to wow her subjects there was no stopping her. Velvet, brocade, satin, silk – you name it, Liz had a dress in it in every colour, studded with gems.

- By the end of her life Elizabeth was rumoured to have 3,000 dresses and 200 cloaks.
- It took her maids two hours to kit her out in her dresses. Perhaps it was because they came in pieces – bodice, sleeves, kirtle, skirt, all worn over a farthingale.

187

- She had a new pair of shoes every week.
- She always wore hand-knitted silk stockings.
- She used to whiten her skin with a mixture of egg-white, powdered egg-shell and borax.

- She washed her hair with wood-ash and water paste.
- She wore so many pearls, diamonds, amber and amethysts that foreign ambassadors wondered how she managed to stay standing.

There were no washing machines in those days and, anyway, Elizabeth's posh frocks weren't the sort you could just sling in the machine. To protect her dresses from sweat, Liz wore an undershift. In fact, Liz was probably a lot cleaner than most of her subjects – she had running water in four of her palaces and a bath she carted round with her when she was away from home. And maybe the reason she almost always ate in private was so she could undress first – or wear a bib!

GOOD QUEEN BESS

Elizabeth was more popular than ever after the Armada, and she had finally won the respect of her own councillors. Lord Burghley declared, 'She is the wisest woman that ever was, for she understands the interests and dispositions of all the princes in her time, and is so perfect in the knowledge of her own realm that no councillor she has can tell her anything she does not know before.'

Even the new Pope was a fan.

She is a great queen and were she only a Catholic, she would be our dearly beloved daughter. Just look how well she governs! She is only a woman, only mistress of half an island, and yet she makes herself feared by Spain, by France, by the Empire, by all! I wish I was free to marry her! What children we would have! They would have ruled the whole world!

It was a great time to be English. Everyone shared in the glory of the Queen. She was in great form, still dancing energetically every day as well as riding, walking, and hunting.

All the same, she wasn't getting any younger and her problems didn't go away:

On top of that, the 1590s were a sad time for her. All her old friends and councillors were getting older too.

Walsingham died in 1590. Blanche Parry, who had been Liz's loyal servant right from the time she was a child, died blind in the same year. Poor old William Cecil, Lord Burghley, was getting on too. He wanted to retire, but Liz wouldn't hear of it, though she did allow him to sit down on a stool in her presence. (Usually everyone had to stand or kneel when she was in the room.)

To cheer herself up, and maybe to make herself feel younger, she decided to make a new conquest. As usual he was dead dishy, and his name was Robert Devereux, Earl of Essex. He was the son of her old enemy, Lettice Knollys.

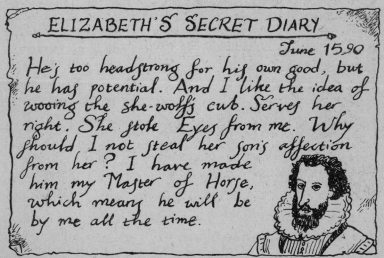

ELIZABETH'S SECRET DIARY

June 1590

He's too headstrong for his own good, but he has potential. And I like the idea of wooing the she-wolf's cub. Serves her right. She stole Eyes from me. Why should I not steal her son's affection from her? I have made him my Master of Horse, which means he will be by me all the time.

The trouble was, Essex didn't want to be by the Queen's side. (She was just a boring old woman to him.) Instead, he wanted to be off having adventures…

Essex's adventures

1 He ran off to join Sir Francis Drake who was sailing to Portugal to support an anti-Spanish prince. Essex was in debt and hoped to capture a Spanish galleon and come home with a lot of money.

Liz was livid, and wrote to Drake telling him to send him back and execute the captain under whom he sailed. (He didn't do either.) The expedition was a complete flop, they didn't capture any ships, thousands of men died of disease, and the Queen lost a lot of money.

2 He fought a duel with Sir Charles Blount, another courtier, because he was jealous the Queen had given Blount a gold chess piece.

Neither man was badly hurt but the Queen was cross because duelling was forbidden.

3 He led an expedition in support of the new Protestant French king, and treated the whole thing like a sporting event. He left his men a hundred miles away and rode into Compiègne dressed in orange velvet covered with jewels, where he held a leaping competition with his French allies. Eventually he had to send for his soldiers to help him get back to base through enemy lines. Then he knighted 24 of his followers.

Liz was outraged. In the end she had spent £300,000 helping the French and she had to sell some crown land to foot the bill. As for making knights – that was *her* prerogative.

4 He sailed with Lord Howard to attack Cadiz in Spain, throwing his hat into the water ahead of the ship, in order to beat Sir Walter Raleigh into the harbour. The English sailors took the town of Cadiz and nicked a lot of Spanish treasure – but Essex let his men keep it. He also made another batch of knights.

Essex was a bad lad, but he was also a national hero. Everyone loved him, especially the new knights and the sailors who had got rich quick. But he was on dangerous ground. Elizabeth liked to be the one who made the conquests. She didn't want any of her subjects to be more popular than she was.

OYEZ OYEZ — HERE IS THE NEWS: ESSEX FOR IRELAND. OYEZ — ESSEX TO TAKE ON TYRONE. NOW OVER TO MY MATE CHARLIE FOR THE WEATHER.

SUNNY INTERVALS AND SCATTERED SHOWERS.

ELIZABETH'S SECRET DIARY

December 1597

Essex got up my nose yesterday, carping about how hopeless our generals are in Ireland. I told him that if he knew so much about it, he should have a go at running the show himself. He is not pleased. Still, it serves him right.

England had ruled a bit of Ireland since the time of Henry II. It was when Elizabeth had started trying to impose anti-Catholic laws in Ireland, however, that the Irish Catholics rose up against her, led by the Earl of Tyrone. Essex was one of a long line of English commanders sent out to sort out the Irish. He made as big a mess of it as everyone else. In fact, some people said he was in league with Tyrone. The Queen kept sending him complaining letters.

> Robert,
> What is the matter with you?
> Why cannot you finish off Tyrone once
> and for all?   I am sick of hearing
> that you are making no progress.
>   ER

One day, Essex had had enough of being wet and cold with no money and thousands of rebels to deal with. He came back from Ireland determined to speak to the Queen.

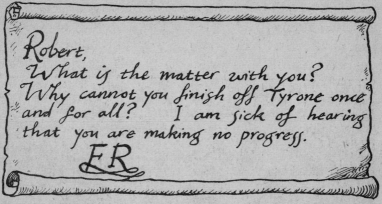

ELIZABETH'S SECRET DIARY

28th September 1599

Dramas, dramas. I was without my wig this morning, just packing my cheeks with muslin, when who should come charging into my bedroom unannounced but Essex – hot, sweaty and muddy from his ride. For a terrible moment I thought he had a troop of men behind him and was come to murder or arrest me.
    I think I did not let him see my fear. I gave him my hand to

kiss, and was civil enough to him. He is angry that I do not appreciate what he does in Ireland, how difficult it is, etc. etc. I spoke soothing words to him, said we should speak later.

After my maids had led him from the room, it became clear that there was no army at his back. But I cannot see him again. He simply does not understand that I am his queen and that he cannot treat me like this. He shall be taught a lesson.

Poor Liz. By this time she was having trouble with her looks. Her teeth were falling out, her hair was getting thin. Because she didn't want anyone to notice, she painted her face and stuffed her cheeks with rags so that she didn't look haggard. She solved the hair problem by wearing red wigs with long curls hanging down her neck. Essex had  burst in on her when she was in her nightdress, with no wig and no make-up. He had seen her as she really was. No wonder there was no meeting for him later that day.

Essex was arrested and kept in prison, and someone new was sent to take over in Ireland. Later, when Essex was ill, Elizabeth forgave him and allowed him to return to his own home, but he was not allowed back to court.

Fall of a favourite

Essex's house was in the Strand in London. Soon, anyone with a grudge against the Queen was popping in to see Essex, from puritans to courtiers...

Liz's spy system was as good as ever. She heard what was going on at Essex House, and sent for Essex and some of his mates to come and explain themselves to the Privy Council.

THE TUDOR TATLER

8 February 1601

ESSEX DEFIES QUEEN

There were dramatic scenes in London today when the Queen's men came to arrest the Earl of Essex, disgraced favourite and darling of the common people. Essex, 34, known for his rashness and bravery, locked the Queen's men out of his house in the Strand, and rode towards Whitehall shouting, 'For the Queen! For the Queen! A plot is laid for my life!' He was followed by a herald who shouted loudly, 'Take no notice! This man is a traitor!'

If the young Earl had been hoping that the people of London would flock to his standard, he was disappointed. A few men seemed willing to follow him, but at the word 'traitor' they slipped quietly away. In the end the Earl went home and barricaded himself in – but the drama wasn't over. As the Queen's troops surrounded his house, Essex could be seen on the roof, shouting and waving his sword at the soldiers below.

Shots were fired and shortly afterwards Essex's wife and a number of other ladies came out of the house to give themselves up, but the Earl still refused to surrender. Then, around 10 pm, gunpowder was brought and laid around the house. At last the Earl saw sense. He came down to the garden where he burnt a number of papers, including a letter from King James of Scotland, which he always wore around his neck. Then, in the dark, he knelt and surrendered his sword.

He was taken to Lambeth Palace from where he will be taken to the Tower of London tomorrow morning.

While Essex was leading his non-rebellion in London, Liz sat quietly eating her lunch.

God has placed me in my seat as a prince, and he will preserve me in it.

The Earl of Essex and some of his fellow-conspirators were both tried for treason and found guilty. Elizabeth expected Essex to plead for his life, but he didn't and so she signed the death warrant. At his own request, Essex had a private execution on 25 February 1601. On the scaffold he swore he had never wanted the Queen's death or intended to lead a coup.

That day Liz sat in her chamber, weeping. She hated executing people and she had once been really fond of Essex. A few of his close friends and conspirators were also executed but to everyone's amazement another conspirator, the Earl of Southampton, was pardoned.

After his death, Essex was more popular than ever. Songs were sung about him, even at court.

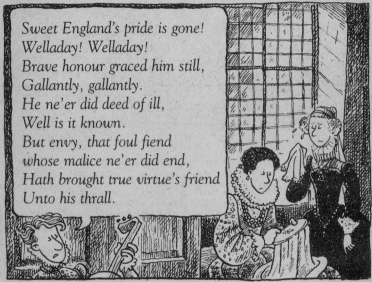

> *Sweet England's pride is gone!*
> *Welladay! Welladay!*
> *Brave honour graced him still,*
> *Gallantly, gallantly.*
> *He ne'er did deed of ill,*
> *Well is it known.*
> *But envy, that foul fiend*
> *whose malice ne'er did end,*
> *Hath brought true virtue's friend*
> *Unto his thrall.*

(In other words, he was a good lad and it was a stitch-up.)

Final days

Elizabeth and her ministers were unpopular because of Essex. Robert Cecil, Lord Burghley's son, was particularly disliked. Liz managed to win back Parliament by repealing the law which hindered free trade, but there was now a feeling that she was getting near the end; she was an old woman. Nevertheless, Liz did everything she could to prove she was still full of life.

ELIZABETH'S SECRET DIARY

March 1601

I can hardly move this morning. People are muttering that I am starting to show my age, so I thought I would give them something to think about. Went for a ten-mile ride yesterday, and then went hunting. A lot of men younger than me were flagging by the end. Trouble is, I am so stiff I can hardly walk today. However, walk I shall. No one shall know that I am tired. No one!

Not only did Liz go for a ten-mile ride and a hunt and followed it with a day's walking, she regularly rode and danced and stayed up half the night talking to her councillors the way she always had.

201

Not even Liz, with all her strength and spirit, could live for ever. The fact is, she was nearly 70 in an age when the average life-expectancy was 35. People knew that when she died there was quite likely to be a struggle for the throne, with the Catholics trying to put the Spanish Infanta or even an English Catholic on the throne. Parliament was desperate for the Queen to name her successor.

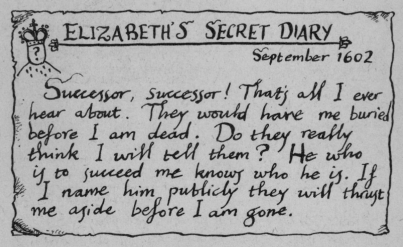

ELIZABETH'S SECRET DIARY

September 1602

Successor, successor! That's all I ever hear about. They would have me buried before I am dead. Do they really think I will tell them? He who is to succeed me knows who he is. If I name him publicly they will thrust me aside before I am gone.

She was in good health right up to February 1603. The Venetian ambassador described her like this:

She was clad in taffeta of silver and white, trimmed with gold. Her dress, somewhat open in the front, showed her throat encircled with pearls and rubies down to her breast. Her skirts were much fuller and began lower down than is the fashion in France. Her hair was of a light colour, never made by nature, and she wore great pearls like pears around the forehead. She had a coif arched around her head and an Imperial crown, and displayed a vast quantity of gems and pearls upon her person. Even under her stomacher, she was covered with golden jewelled girdles and single gems, carbuncles, balas-rubies, diamonds; round her wrists, in place of bracelets, she wore double rows of pearls of more than medium size. She stood throughout our interviews and spoke to me in fluent Italian.

Then came another plot to get rid of her and put another distant cousin, Arabella Stewart, on the throne. Elizabeth was hurt and upset.

ELIZABETH'S SECRET DIARY

November 16??

More plots. Will they never end? I think not. They know that I am old and think to help me to my grave. Arabella was always a spoilt and

Silly girl, but it will mean more axeings and that I do not like.

My finger is swollen. My coronation ring is too tight now, it cuts into my flesh. My physician says there is no help but to cut it off.

Is it an omen?

In March 1603, the court moved to Richmond. Liz was still depressed about Essex, and now young Arabella. She became very ill, as her lady-in-waiting, Lady Scrope told her brother...

16th March 1603

My brother Robert,

I write to you because I believe it may soon be time for you to make your long ride north, and so I warn you to get your horses ready. Our Sovereign Lady has throat ulcers and chest pains which I think may be pneumonia. For days she has sat on cushions staring into the fire, never eating, hardly speaking; and when she does, it is all of Essex and Arabella.

Then, yesterday, she ordered us to raise her to her feet. There she stood, brother, feverish and swaying, for fifteen hours. And we stood too, for as you know, no one may sit while the Queen stands. I thought I should collapse. I longed to help my poor Lady back to her cushions, or at least to a chair, but I durst not speak, and neither durst anyone else, for fear of rousing her temper.

I had really thought we might stand through the night, but God took mercy on us, and our Sovereign Lady fainted clean away.

She was helped back to her cushions, where I think she is failing fast. Pray be ready on a fast horse beneath the window, and the moment she breathes her last I will drop her sapphire ring down to you that you may take it post-haste to the King of Scotland.

Your loving sister,

Eleanor

All Liz's leading councillors and courtiers were agreed at this point that James was the rightful heir to the English throne. Robert Cecil had been in secret communication with him for years. Yet Elizabeth herself had never come out and said James was her successor. Now, as she lay dying on cushions in front of a fire, her councillors tried for the last time to get an answer from her.

Trouble me no more. Who else but my cousin Scotland?

So, at last it was definite. Liz's councillors were ready. It was important that James received the news and came to London as quickly as possible to forestall a Catholic coup.

The Queen is dead – long live the King

Seven strong, fast horses were ready at fifty-mile intervals up the Great North Road. Sir Robert Carey, dressed for a long cold ride, sat astride his own horse, beneath the window of the Queen's withdrawing room. In the early hours of 23rd March 1603, his sister, Lady Scrope, appeared at the Queen's bedroom window and silently dropped the sapphire ring from Liz's finger down to him. The Queen had drawn her last breath. Sir Robert caught it and was off, riding like the wind. He covered the four hundred miles to Edinburgh in three days. James, King of Scots, was now James I of England.

THE TUDOR TATLER
29 April 1603
FAREWELL DEAR LADY

Huge crowds gathered in London yesterday to say farewell to the noble lady who has been our Queen for 45 years. So thick were the crowds that the Knight's Marshal's men had to clear a path for the procession.

The lead coffin containing the Queen's body was drawn by four horses decked in black. Covered in purple velvet, there was a life-size effigy on it of the Queen in her robes of state and royal crown. Six earls carried a canopy to protect the coffin. Then came the Queen's Master of Horse, leading her favourite palfrey. Many people wept when they saw the familiar horse without its rider. Next, dressed in black, came the chief mourners led by the Marchioness of Northampton. All the ladies of the court and many peeresses of the realm walked behind the coffin through the streets to Westminster Abbey. Behind them walked 260 poor women, four abreast.

A real eyewitness at the funeral that day wrote this:

Westminster was surcharged with multitudes of all sorts of people in the streets, houses, windows, leads and gutters, that came to see the funeral, and when they beheld her statue lying upon the coffin, there was such a general sighing, groaning and weeping as the like hath not been seen or known in the memory of man, neither doth any history mention any people, time or state to make like lamentation for the death of their sovereign.

The Age of Elizabeth was over. It had seen daring sea-captains and ambitious soldiers; solid statesmen and showy courtiers; poets, playwrights and musicians whose work is famous to this day. In the midst of them all was a queen encrusted with jewels who could lose her temper in Latin, hold her own with the philosophers of the day, ride, hunt and dance energetically, and still take the time to go and spoon-feed her faithful Sir Spirit, Lord Burghley, when he lay dying.

She was going to be a hard act to follow. Nevertheless, she was gone. The Elizabethan Age was over and the Jacobean Age was about to begin.